CHILE PEPPER FEVER

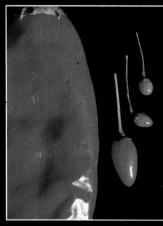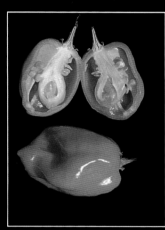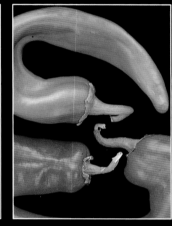

MINE'S HOTTER THAN YOURS

TEXT BY
SUSAN HAZEN-HAMMOND

PHOTOGRAPHS BY
EDUARDO FUSS

GRAMERCY BOOKS
New York • Avenel

This 1996 edition is published by Gramercy Books,
a division of Random House Value Publishing, Inc.,
40 Engelhard Avenue, Avenel, New Jersey 07001,
by arrangement with Voyageur Press.

Gramercy Books and colophon are trademarks of
Random House Value Publishing, Inc.

Random House
New York • Toronto • London • Sydney • Auckland
http://www.randomhouse.com/

Edited by Kathryn Mallien

Printed in China

Library of Congress Cataloging-in-Publication Data
Hazen-Hammond, Susan.
Chile pepper fever / by Susan Hazen-Hammond.
p. cm.
Originally published: Stillwater, MN, U.S.A.: Voyageur Press, c. 1993.
Includes bibliographical references (p.   ) and index.
ISBN 0-517-18254-8 (hardcover)
1. Hot peppers. 2. Cookery (Hot peppers) I. Title.
[SB307.P4H39 1996]
641.3'384—dc20   96-5795   CIP

8 7 6 5 4 3 2 1

TO WILLIAM,
who will never forget the day the Habaneros almost ate him.

Chile peppers—all members of the genus *Capsicum*—don't just create hot dishes. They create hot opinions. Capsicum lovers often disagree about the correct name of any given pepper. They also argue about the spelling of the word *chile,* and about whether the fruits should be called chiles, peppers, or chile peppers. The quibbling is part of the fun. Metaphorically, peppers provide a chance for the plant world and human beings to enjoy a laugh together.

CONTENTS

ε ε ε

"Unless they have chiles, they think they're not eating."
—BARTOLOMÉ DE LAS CASAS, 1552

There's more to peppers than eating them, as these Mirasol chiles from Mexico illustrate. Florists sometimes display sprigs of colorful chiles between more conventional bouquets of daisies and roses.

INTRODUCTION:
The Berry that Bites Back

 ONE DAY ABOUT TEN THOUSAND YEARS AGO, WHEN THE WORLD was old enough to be peopled but too young to be filled with grocery stores, one of our forerunners in the Americas strayed into unfamiliar countryside, looking for food. This is just a guess, but suppose that as she stood near the edge of a stream, hungrily fingering her empty food pouch, she noticed a bird devouring tiny red fruits on a leafy bush that grew under a tree.

Our foremother had never tasted these glistening round berries, but hunger and experience convinced her that if birds could eat them, people could, too. She took a bite.

Instantly, her eyes watered, her nose ran, sweat poured down her face, and her mouth felt as if a volcano had erupted inside it. Lips first, she dived into the stream, promising the gods that if she survived, she would never, ever try an unknown food again.

But when she came up for air, the first human being to eat a chile pepper felt a pleasant tingling inside. Maybe those explosive berries were worth a second try.

She reached out for another, then another. Then she hurried off to tell her friends, and humankind took another zigzag step along the double helix—downward path, upward spiral—that leads to culinary wisdom.

Ten thousand years later, I mentioned to my sister-in-law in Buenos Aires, Argentina, that I was writing a long essay about chile peppers. She and many other Latin Americans know peppers by their Arawak Indian name, *ají*.

"Ají?" The astonishment in her voice came through clearly over the long-distance phone lines. "You're writing a book about ají?"

I started to explain the rationale. Extravagant accounts of the provocative pod's medicinal, gustatory, and aphrodisiacal powers come from every continent. Like a top-drawing movie or leading comic-strip character, peppers have spawned fan clubs, magazines, cookbooks, cookoffs, and lookalike byproducts—more than any other food. Chiles are said to engender more puns, metaphors, and practical jokes than all the rest of the plant kingdom combined. Probably there has never been a vegetable in all the history of humankind that more people have argued about, sworn at, praised, lied about, and made claims for than chile peppers.

My sister-in-law wasn't listening. She was remembering. "You should have been here the time Papá stopped by the florist's to get some flowers. He came home with the most beautiful plant we'd ever seen, lots of pretty little buds, red, yellow, orange, green. We kept waiting for them to blossom. It took weeks before we finally figured out those weren't buds at all, and that plant wasn't a flower."

She chortled. "It was ají. You know, those really hot ones: the Putaparió."

Other fruits and vegetables provide a meal and pass from memory. Not peppers. They grab the senses. They make us laugh. They make us cry. They make us think. They make us remember. They connect us to other people. They make us feel human. They make us feel alive. And the way we interact with chiles tells us about ourselves.

Chiles also turn us into storytellers. Talk to practically any Chilehead, as chile aficionados are called. They'll tell you story after story about their experiences with peppers, which have been called both "grains of paradise" and "bullets from hell."

Every Chilehead, it seems, has a story that could be titled "The Hottest One I Ever Tasted." Botanist W. Hardy Eshbaugh, of Oxford, Ohio, who has spent three decades collecting and analyzing chiles, recalls one of his visits to Bolivia. He was hunting along hillsides and valleys for wild species of *Capsicum*, the genus to which all chiles belong. "One day, I picked up a pepper half the size of my fingernail and squeezed a drop onto my tongue. It was so hot, I couldn't talk for five minutes."

Paul McIlhenny is vice president of the McIlhenny Company, which makes the world's best-known chile product, Tabasco brand pepper sauce. He still remembers the Bird's Eye peppers that grew in his family's yard in New Orleans, Louisiana, when he was a boy. They were small, shiny, fiery hot, and they looked like candy. "One day my twin sister gave one of those little red peppers to a friend and told him it was a piece of red hot candy," he reminisces. When the boy bit into the pepper, he howled and spit it out. McIlhenny, 49, laughs to remember that moment four decades ago and says, "He's still afraid of us today."

Texans Hill Rylander, who runs the Travis County Farmers' Market, and Ignacio "Nacho" Padilla, president of the El Paso Farmers' Market Association, could talk nonstop for a week about what is being called the Great Chile War between Texas and New Mexico. The goal of the whacky war, says Rylander, is to alert Texas farmers to what they're missing by allowing New Mexicans to be the number-one chile producers in the United States. Recalling one skirmish, Padilla says, "We stuffed a cannon full of Texas long green chiles and fired it at New Mexico." Adds Rylander, "Those New Mexicans just laughed at us and said, 'Ha. Ha. You missed.'"

Some chile stories portray real life-and-death incidents. Gloria Lomahaftewa, a Hopi Indian, works as a curator at the Heard Museum in Phoenix, Arizona. She remembers Hopi meals in which she and her family dipped Hopi blue-corn bread into the grease in which chiles had been fried. Sometimes older family members would relate the tale of how their people punished the villagers of Awátovi, who welcomed the Spanish back to Hopi country following the Pueblo revolt of 1680: "When they knew the men of Awátovi were down in the kiva having a ceremony, they threw hot chiles onto the fire in the kiva. Then they sealed the kiva up, and the people inside died." Concludes Lomahaftewa with a sigh, "It was the only time in Hopi history when Hopis killed each other."

Most Chileheads remember their first encounters with chiles almost as vividly as their first experiences with sex.

My own first taste of powdered fire came when I was four. My mother had taken me from our home in Montana to visit my grandparents in Maine. Poking around my grandmother's kitchen cupboard one day, I found a glass spice bottle about five inches high and an inch in diameter. It contained chile powder.

One look set my mother and grandmother to talking. This bottle, it turned out, had stood fifty years on my great-grandmother and grandmother's shelves. In all that time, they used only the top inch of spice. The granules faded from red to brownish yellow, but they kept their zing. Occasionally, when Grandma wanted to add life to a kettle of New England fish chowder or boiled dinner, she would drop in a grain or two of powder. But rarely more. One time when he thought she had used too much, my grandfather threatened to feed the whole bottle to the woodchuck that grew fat every year in his garden.

While the women talked, I unscrewed the heavy metal cap and stuck my fingers into the powder.

"You'd better not touch that," my grandmother warned. "That stuff bites back."

My mother dived for me.

I plunged my fingers into my mouth.

As the granules warmed my tongue, my first reaction was startled delight. But my grandmother and mother had already given me enough clues so that I knew the appropriate response. After the briefest pause to savor the heat, I made a face and spit the powder out.

Since then, I've sampled dozens of varieties of peppers, and have wound my way through life on such a different culinary path from my grandmother that I sympathize with the sixteenth-century Mexicans about whom Bartolomé de las Casas wrote, "Unless they have chiles, they think they're not eating." But a part of me retains the astonishment I felt four decades ago when Grandma's chile powder first bit my tongue. And every time I taste an especially hot chile, I feel connected to that first daredevil chile eater ten thousand years ago.

My partner and husband, photographer Eduardo Fuss, grew up in Buenos Aires, where local cuisine seldom featured anything more potent than black pepper. Like other Buenos Aires housewives, his Polish-born mother used no more chile powder in her cooking than my grandmother did. But as a child he heard stories about explosively hot chiles named after a strong oath. It was said that anyone who tried to eat them began swearing violently, "What whore gave birth to you?" It was these blistering peppers that my sister-in-law remembers as an ornamental plant: the Putaparió.

Today, Eduardo eats chiles even more enthusiastically than I do, and he loves to tell about the time he took a bite of really hot chile, when he first visited Santa Fe, New Mexico, in 1978. A Pueblo Indian woman was selling fried meat pies called *empanadas* out of a basket on the plaza. "It was good," he says, "picante, but good. And then I took the last bite. It contained enough chiles for an entire year's worth of empanadas. I thought I was going to have to have reconstructive surgery on my mouth."

But what Eduardo really likes about chiles is their visual appeal. It intrigues him that they come in so many shapes, colors, and sizes, and that their skins shine as if nature had shellacked them. "I especially like the small varieties," he says. "Through the camera lens, they look like jewels."

I was already hooked on peppers. But it was Eduardo's love of the visual poetry of chiles, and the enthusiasm with which readers of *Smithsonian* and other magazines responded to his photos, that made me take a second look at the lore and literature of peppers. Jean Andrews, Dave DeWitt, Nancy Gerlach, Janet Long-Solís, Amal Naj, and others had already written insightfully and well about chiles. But there was still so much to say. No one had ever written at any length about chile peppers and their connection to popular culture. No chile writer had ever noticed tidbits like Swiss-born Philipp Segesser's 1737 recipe for chili stew, or Frenchman Jean-Bernard Bossu's pepperpowered culinary adventures among the Indians of Alabama in the mid-1700s. Above all, no one had ever photographed chiles the way Eduardo had photographed them, or combined such photos into a book of art photography that included a meaty text.

The words and pictures in this book are for all present and potential pepper eaters: from those who imagine that the word *Habanero* is an incantation in an exotic language to those who can recite every anecdote and legend that has ever appeared in that quintessential catalog of chile lore, *Chile Pepper* magazine.

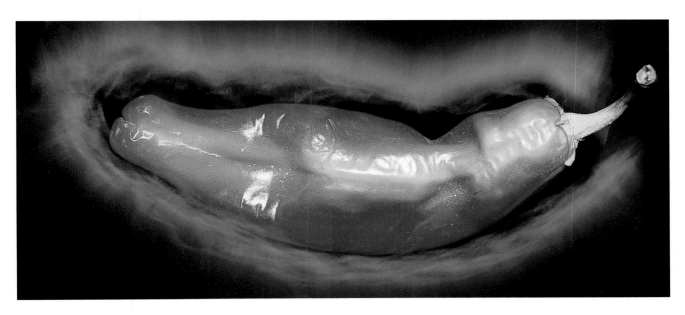

§ § §

> "Its pungency is so great, that, amongst the uninitiated,
> it produces absolute excoriation."
> —H.G. WARD, ESQ., 1828

For decades, the men and women of Siberia have grown potted peppers indoors on their window ledges so that during the long, frozen winter, they can warm their bellies with fiery stews. Dubbed simply "Siberians," these blazing *Capsicum annuums* taste and look much like the peppers from Thailand that are known in English as Thai Hots.

MINE'S HOTTER THAN YOURS:
An Overview of Chiles

LIKE STARS OR HUMAN BEINGS, NO TWO PEPPERS ARE EVER totally alike. In theory, they come in more than a trillion combinations of sizes, shapes, colors, tastes, and degrees of piquancy. In practice, they separate out into approximately two thousand distinctive varieties.

No one knows more about that diversity than Paul Bosland, associate professor of horticulture at New Mexico State University (NMSU) in Las Cruces, whom journalists from the United States and beyond dub "The Chileman." In his greenhouses and test plots, Bosland, a wiry blond man with an easy smile, plants more than one thousand different varieties of peppers each spring.

One year late in August, Eduardo and I went with Bosland out to a sampler plot where he had planted more than one hundred varieties of chiles in miniplots of half a dozen plants each.

Chiles in various stages of ripening glistened among the bushy leaves. Some were still green. Others gleamed orange, yellow, purple, black, white, or the predominant color for mature chiles: red. The bushes resembled green fiesta skirts dotted with color.

We passed chiles that look like large cherries but are called Cascabel, because, when dried, they sound like a baby's rattle or a rattlesnake's tail. Nearby grew chiles that are sometimes called Mirasol because they grow straight up towards the sun and sometimes called Elephant's Trunk because they look a bit like an elephant's trunk trumpeting towards the sky. Beyond them grew long, ridged chiles from South America that go by the vague general name Ají.

We saw half a dozen kinds of fleshy Jalapeños, including the TAM Mild Jalapeño-1, which plant breeder Ben Villalon of Texas A&M University developed in the 1970s for people who want to eat Jalapeños but don't like spicy foods. We passed curving Cayenne

peppers that make the hottest Jalapeños seem mild, and tiny, oblong Thai Hots that taste even more fiery. We saw everyday chiles like the Serrano, a common ingredient in the foods of northern Mexico, and the Poblano, a broad chile that can be served stuffed with cheese, meat, and rice. We passed exotic chiles like the Gambo, which looks like a giant raisin when it dries, and Holiday Cheer, an ornamental whose fruits resemble Christmas cranberries.

Finally we stopped in front of a spindly cluster of half a dozen plants that rose roughly two feet above the ground. The plants in other miniplots all around us produced only one variety of chile per plot. But here a different kind of pepper hung down among the leaves of each plant. Some were skinny, about an inch and a half long. Others were fatter and longer. A few thick, wrinkled fruits, about four inches long, were unmistakably Peter peppers, so-called because they resemble male anatomy.

Bosland broke open a long, slender red chile that appeared to be a type of Cayenne and handed part of it to me. I took a careful taste. "Hot, but nothing compared to the Chile Hots that grow in Missouri," I ventured.

Bosland, who has the wholesome look of an award-winning Boy Scout leader, grinned. "I was playing the old pepper eaters' trick on you," he said, showing me what he had in his hand. He had saved the mild, lower outer wall of the chile for himself and handed me the hottest part, containing the ribs and seeds.

"These are Pili-Pili from Africa," he continued. "That's a generic term. They could be one of several different species of *Capsicum*. That's the problem with common names."

From there we moved on to a row of long, thick red chiles, the kind that show up each autumn in grocery stores around the Southwest and beyond. "Take these chiles," he said. "Some people call them Anaheims. A few still call them Texas Long Greens or New Mexico Long Greens."

I mentioned that farm workers I'd talked to in California called them Californios.

"I've never heard that one," he said. "But the point is, they grew in New Mexico long before farmers started planting them in California or Texas. Their correct name is New Mexico, or New Mexico 6–4 chiles."

Bosland laughed. "I'm beginning to sound like all the people who contact me with questions about chiles. They want everything to fit neatly into a box. Chiles don't, and people who try to do that can end up feeling terribly frustrated."

Just how many boxes chiles won't fit into becomes obvious when you realize that people can't even agree on the correct spelling of the word. Alternatives include *chilli, chilley, chillie, chilie, chili,* and even *chilly.* For clarity, many people, including me, use the spelling *chile* to designate the plant and its fruit and *chili* to refer to a stew made from chiles or chile powders.

Other vagaries include the collective name: What general word should we use for all these brightly colored pods, which are not just a fruit, but a berry, and which we also eat as a vegetable, a condiment, and a spice? Should we call them peppers? Chiles? Chile peppers? Ají? Capsicums? "There is no one right answer," says Ohio chile expert W. Hardy Eshbaugh. "It's all of the above. Strictly speaking, it's correct to call even Bell peppers *chiles.* But some people get excited. Heaven knows. They think if you call it a chile pepper, it's got to be hot." Other people, I've discovered, save the word *chiles* for New Mexico peppers and use the term *peppers* for everything else.

Many people prefer the general term *peppers.* One drawback with that, though, is the potential confusion with black pepper, *Piper nigrum,* to which chiles are not related. It's as if, by some quirk of linguistic history, we had managed to call both human beings and, say, trout, by one name: *people.*

Personally, I like to use the terms *chiles, chile peppers,* and *peppers* interchangeably. And, although it makes the dormant English teacher in me twitch, I follow the practice of those chile scholars who capitalize the names of particular chiles.

Botanists agree that the first chile plant grew in South America, uncounted millennia ago, but they debate its exact geographic origins. Some researchers, like Eshbaugh, think chiles may have originated in or near Bolivia. Others suggest Brazil. Chile scholar Barbara Pickersgill of the Department of Agriculture at Reading University in Reading, England, says, "At this point our evidence is so sketchy that we simply have to be prepared to be proven wrong. I believe they originated south of the equator, probably around the margins of

Left to their own, chiles cross-breed enthusiastically. Most farmers prevent that. But Bob Kennedy, who grows twenty varieties of peppers in the Virgin Islands for use in his Virgin Fire hot sauces, lets his peppers mix and match at will. "I end up with some surprising combinations of color, shape, and heat," he says, "but most of the hybrids are vigorous and prolific." In the plots shown here, at New Mexico State University in Las Cruces, plant breeder Paul Bosland has covered his chile plants with netting to prevent them from cross-pollinating the way Kennedy's peppers do.

Amazonia. But there's still so much we don't know."

Botanists also argue about the dividing lines among species in the genus *Capsicum*. Some, like Paul Smith, the father of American pepper genetics and professor emeritus at the University of California at Davis, argue that domesticated Capsicums fall into five species: *Capsicum annuum, C. pubescens, C. baccatum, C. frutescens,* and *C. chinense.* Others, like Hardy Eshbaugh, say *frutescens* and *chinense* are one species, not two. Still others suggest that both *frutescens* and *chinense* may actually be *annuums,* which already account for more varieties than all other species combined.

Pickersgill shrugs. "It's a matter of judgment and subjective opinion what you do with that." Such arguments reflect the struggle between two camps: the "lumpers" and the "splitters."

People sometimes break each species down further into pod types. But lumpers refer to fifty pod types or fewer, and splitters talk about hundreds, or even thousands. So these distinctions have limited value. Worse yet, any given variety of peppers may have a dozen different common names.

Even the exact boundaries of the genus *Capsicum* are in doubt. Partly because of that, and partly because some species remain to be identified, no one knows how many wild species exist—probably fewer than thirty.

Next to Paul Bosland's sampler plots stands his three-thousand-square-foot greenhouse. When the sun grew too hot outdoors, we retreated there.

ABSOLUTELY NO SMOKING, said a sign. Huge fans on either side of the door sucked air through the greenhouse with a whir so loud we had to shout. Water dripped onto pads along the back wall, and it felt as if we were standing inside a giant swamp cooler.

Bosland sprayed his hands with alcohol and handed the bottle to me. "This reduces the risk of bringing in some kinds of plant disease," he explained. "For instance, chiles are so closely related to tobacco botanically that tobacco viruses can be transmitted to them just by smoking near a plant, or just by touching a cigarette and then touching a plant."

Eduardo looked at his hands. A long-time smoker, he had never imagined that he was serving as a commuter train for plant viruses.

An aisle ran lengthwise down the greenhouse, with rows of tables on either side. About five hundred pots of pepper plants covered the tables. Some plants grew barely half a foot high; others rose more than three feet tall.

Only a number identified each plant, but Bosland knew them all by their botanical and common names. "This is an example of *Capsicum pubescens,*" he said, holding up a Manzana chile, which resembles a small apple. "The average person probably wouldn't be able to tell it's not a *Capsicum annuum.* In fact, even a botanist might have a hard time, just by seeing the whole fruit. But there's one easy way to check." He pulled out a pocket knife and sliced the chile open. Inside, the seeds looked much like the seeds of a Bell pepper, except that they were black; those seeds distinguish *Capsicum pubescens* from other domesticated Capsicums.

Bosland touched his tongue cautiously to the chile, then grimaced and pulled back. "I've heard that in South America they call *pubescens* Kill-a-Gringo chile or Raise-the-Dead chile. It's easy to see why."

On other tables grew *Capsicum baccatum,* another pungent South American species whose varieties include the Putaparió of Eduardo's childhood and the long orange Ajís we'd seen outside. Nearby grew a bright red variety of *Capsicum frutescens,* commonly known as the Tabasco pepper. That half-inch oblong of gustatory dynamite gives McIlhenny Tabasco sauce its zip and distinguishes Tabasco sauce from other Louisiana-style hot sauces, which generally use Cayenne. On another table grew a slender, emaciated looking orange chile, a type of *Capsicum chinense,* which grows primarily in the Caribbean, the Yucatan, Brazil, and Africa. On another sat several different varieties of Paprika peppers from Central Europe, all *Capsicum annuums.* Some of the Paprikas resembled Poblano chiles. Others looked like tomatoes.

Many of the greenhouse chiles were wild peppers, which may grow oblong or round, but always remain small. Bosland stopped at a plant with fuzzy leaves and pea-sized green fruits. "This species grows wild in the Galapagos Islands," he said. "It may soon be extinct, outside greenhouses. Yet genetically it's a critical chile because it may carry a gene that makes it salt tolerant." By crossing this species, called *Capsicum galapagoense* or *galapogensis,* with other chiles, Bosland and other breeders may be able to produce a cultivar that

For more than a century, horticulturists at New Mexico State University have tailored chiles to the tastes and needs of food processors, farmers, consumers, and tourists. Like his best-known predecessors—Fabian Garcia, Roy Harper, and Roy Nakayama—Paul Bosland has become a link between the public and the esoteric world of plant genetics. Observes the easygoing horticulturist, "My parents' friends think it's a little odd that someone actually gets paid to do what I do."

��ᲑᲚᲐᲑᲔ

PIQUANCY: THREE PEPPERS

STARTER CHILI STEW

2 cloves garlic
1 onion
2 Tablespoons olive or canola oil
1 pound of raw beef, pork, venison, rabbit, or other
   meat
2 Tablespoons hot *chile molido* (chiles ground into
   powder)
3 Tablespoons mild paprika powder
2 Tablespoons flour
3 cups cold water
salt and black pepper to taste

Mince the garlic and onion and sauté in oil in a two-quart saucepan. Cut the meat into small cubes, approximately 1/4-inch on each side, and add to the onion mixture. Cook over medium heat, stirring frequently, until meat has browned well. Add *chile molido* and paprika powder and continue cooking over low heat, stirring frequently. Mix the flour well into two tablespoons of the cold water until free of lumps; add another two tablespoons of water and blend well. Pour the flour mixture into the remaining water and stir well. Add to the meat mixture. Add salt and black pepper to taste and simmer over low heat for two hours, stirring often. Serves two or three.

   Some people spend a lifetime tinkering with their chili recipes. Possible additions to this starter recipe include tomato paste or puréed tomatoes, minced Bell peppers (red or green), fresh Serranos or Jalapeños, dried Japonés chiles, oregano, cumin, cornmeal, and spices such as allspice, cloves, mace, marjoram, nutmeg, or cinnamon.

As they ripen, these tiny *Capsicum baccatum* peppers and other wild chiles grow mushy and fall away easily from their stems. Such traits may have developed through wild chiles' interactions with birds. Birds prefer soft fruits to firm fruits, and they find it easier to eat a fruit that pulls away from the stem. So they leave firmer peppers and those with tight stems to rot on the plant. After the birds have eaten the peppers they prefer, they spread the seeds in their droppings, creating a natural form of genetic selection.

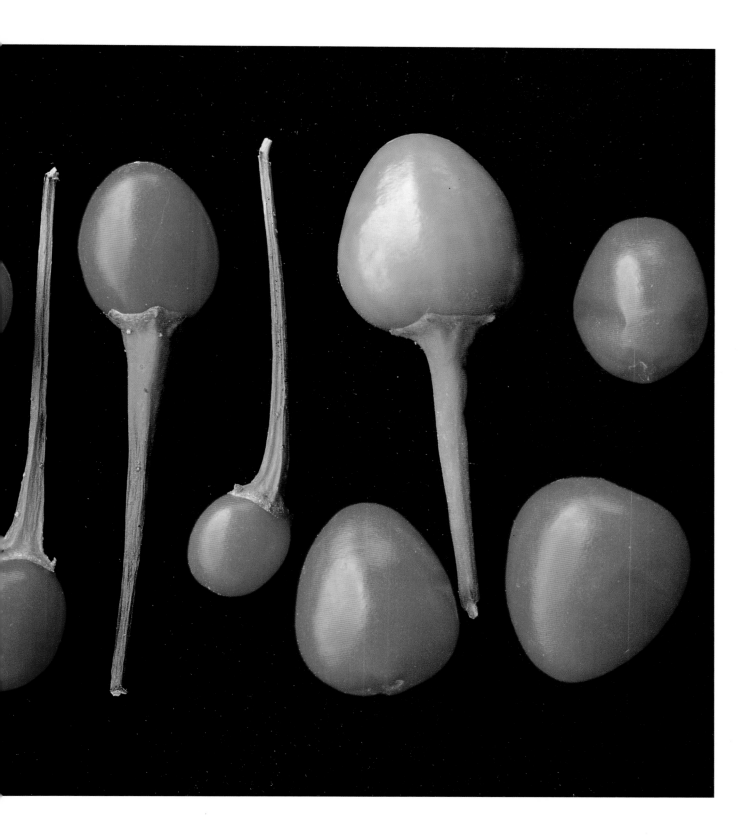

Above: Compounds called capsaicinoids produce the heat that makes peppers famous. Capsaicinoids concentrate in the cross walls of the fruit and travel in the yellow-orange droplets seen in this Jalapeño. Removing the seeds and ribs reduces the heat of a pepper; Mexicans call this procedure castration. They name the hollow chiles that remain Capones, a word that also describes neutered animals.

Left: Throughout Latin America, the name *ají* applies to any type of chile pepper, regardless of species. Even Bells are sometimes called *ají dulce* (sweet peppers). In the United States, some chile writers restrict the term *ají* to one species, *Capsicum baccatum*. The chiles shown here, a variety of *Capsicum chinense*, grow in Peru, where people call them simply Brown Ají.

survives in salty soil.

People from all over the world send Bosland chile seeds and chile questions. "The number one question is always, 'Which chile is the hottest on earth?'"

As die-hard Chileheads know, the burning sensation that makes chiles so appealing to culinary thrill-seekers comes from capsaicin, or, more accurately, a collection of compounds called capsaicinoids. These develop in the placenta, or cross-ribs, of the fruit, which is why that part of the chile is the hottest. A single dominant gene transmits capsaicinoids. Bell peppers are *Capsicum annuums* just like Jalapeños, Serranos, Thai Hots, and most other hot peppers you might find in a grocery store. But Bells taste bland instead of pungent because they lack that gene.

You can't smell most capsaicinoids, and apart from their bite, most have no taste. But they're so potent that some tasters have reported they could detect capsaicinoids in a solution containing only one part per thirty million.

Early in this century, a pharmacist named Wilbur Scoville devised a way of scoring capsaicinoid content: Scoville Units. Most peppers fall into a range from zero to 300,000 Scoville Units. Bell peppers rate zero because they contain no capsaicinoids. Mild peppers like New Mexico 6–4s earn 500 to 1,000 units. Jalapeños measure 2,500 to 5,000. Both Tabasco peppers and Cayennes rank 30,000 to 50,000. Wild Chiltepíns receive 50,000 to 100,000 units. At the top end, peppers like the Caribbean's Scotch Bonnet and the Yucatan's Habanero earn up to 300,000.

These days many chile writers use a new system, the Official Chile Heat Scale, with a rating of zero to ten. Bell

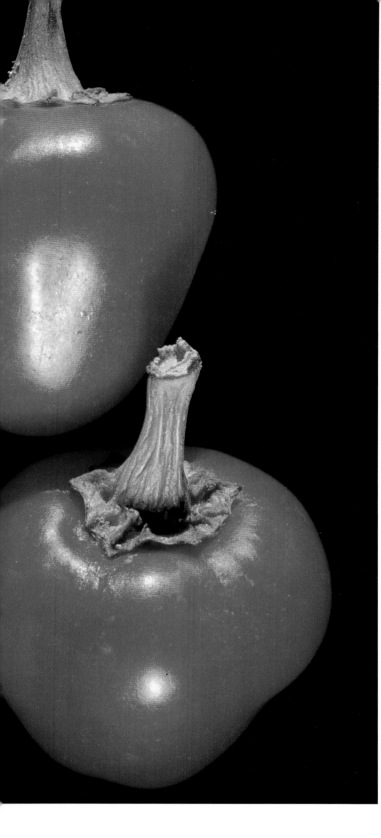

peppers still fall to the bottom, with zero; Scotch Bonnets and Habaneros still fly to the top, with ten. In between come Jalapeños at five, Serranos at six, Cayennes and Tabascos at eight, and wild Chiltepíns at nine.

Both ratings sound scientific enough, but both rely on nothing more precise than the perceptions of the tasters.

If you and I sat down together and tested ten different peppers, we might not agree on a single one. Dave DeWitt, editor of *Chile Pepper* magazine and co-author of *The Whole Chile Pepper Book,* says Jalapeños taste hotter to him than Habaneros, even though the Habanero earns fifty to one hundred times more Scoville Units and is twice as hot on the Official Chile Heat Scale. Personally, I find Thai Hots noticeably hotter than Chiltepíns, even though they rate the same.

Science offers an answer, of sorts, in the high performance liquid chromatography (HPLC) machine. In a crowded laboratory at New Mexico State University, research specialist Peggy Collins, a fair-haired woman in a white lab coat, showed us how she uses this $35,000 machine.

The process starts with chiles, fresh in from the fields. "We dry them in our drying ovens at about 55 to 60 degrees centigrade," Peggy said. "That takes from two to five days. When you can reach in and crush them, they're dry. Then we grind them, being careful to take the grinder apart and clean it between each sample." Work-study students bag and label the powder.

After that Collins mixes the powder with a solvent and cooks it for four hours at 80 degrees centigrade. "That extracts the capsaicinoids from the powder," she explained. "Afterwards, we filter any solids out, and this is what we get." She reached into a cupboard and pulled out a small vial. It contained about an inch and a half of orange-colored liquid.

Texas scholar-artist Jean Andrews set the standard for all chile writers in her 1984 book *Peppers: The Domesticated Capsicums.* While researching, she discovered a gardening dictionary by Englishman Phillip Miller, who described his era's version of a pepper practical joke: "Some mix the powder with snuff to give others diversion." Miller didn't recommend this, however, because "it causes violent fits of sneezing to break the blood vessels of the head, as I have observed of some to whom it has been given." Sweet varieties of the Red Cherry peppers shown here wouldn't produce such an effect, but hot varieties might.

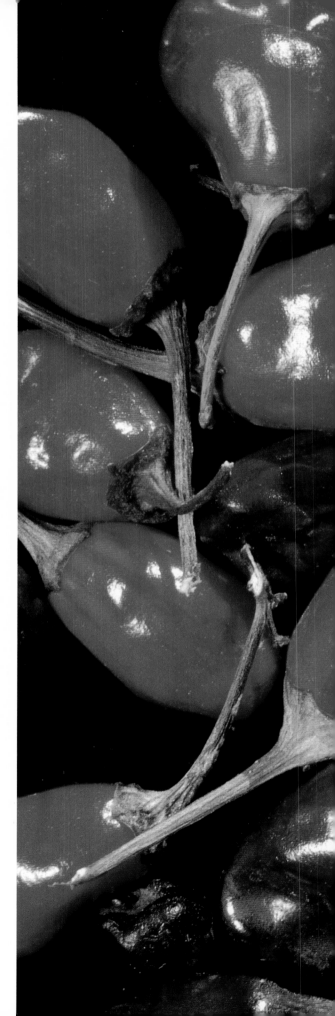

PIQUANCY: ONE PEPPER

BALLS OF· FIRE (MEATBALLS)

2 slices of dry French bread
approximately 1/4 cup milk
1 pound ground sirloin
1 onion
1 fresh Jalapeño pepper
2 Tablespoons olive or canola oil
1 egg or two egg whites
2 ounces grated Parmesan cheese
approximately 2 teaspoons chopped fresh cilantro
1/2 teaspoon salt
1/4 teaspoon coarse-grind black pepper
canola oil for frying

Soak the bread in the milk, squeeze it lightly, and add to the sirloin, discarding any extra milk. Chop the onion fine. Using rubber gloves, wash the Jalapeño, remove and discard the stem, and chop the pepper extra fine. Open all the windows in the kitchen and sauté the onion and Jalapeño lightly in the oil. (If the fumes bother you, cover the pan; if they still bother you, consider the mixture sautéed enough.) Cool slightly and add to the meat mixture, blending well. Beat the egg lightly and add Parmesan, cilantro, salt, and black pepper. Add this mixture to the meat mixture and blend together well.

Wearing rubber gloves, form the meat mixture into balls approximately one inch in diameter and separate the balls into two batches. Pour oil into a cast-iron skillet so that half an inch of oil covers the bottom. Heat until a piece of meat mixture dropped in the oil sizzles. Turn heat to medium high and fry the first batch of meatballs until the underside is brown. Roll them over so that the other side cooks. Remove from the oil with a slotted spoon and drain well on paper towels. Fry the second batch of meatballs in the same oil. Makes approximately forty-two meatballs.

These mildly hot meatballs make excellent appetizers and may be served with Sizzling Salsa (page 60) as a dip. They also go well in homemade or canned spaghetti sauces. As appetizers, they taste best if served within two hours of cooking.

To make zippier meatballs, add an additional Jalapeño.

Like a cook creating a twist in a piece of pastry, nature has added a crinkle to the end of each of these Jigsaw peppers. Hobbyists develop many ornamental *Capsicum annuums* like these, but few ornamentals become widely available.

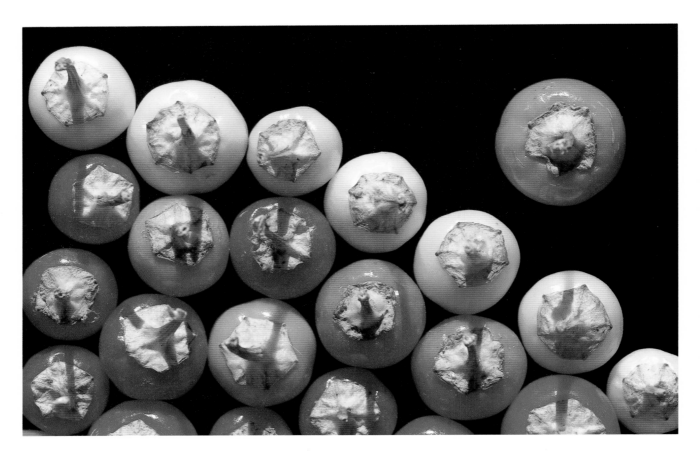

When plant breeder Paul Smith began studying chile peppers in the 1940s, most writers lumped all domesticated Capsicums into one species: *Capsicum frutescens*. Smith analyzed their flowers, crossability, and other features and concluded there were five domesticated species. Today other pepper breeders honor the retired University of California professor as the father of American pepper genetics. But they continue to debate the exact number of domesticated species. Here, ornamental *Capsicum annuum* peppers called Holiday Cheer frustrate those who classify chiles neatly into pod types.

Known simply as Chile Blanco because of their white color, these peppers grow in the Caribbean. Like most other nonengineered varieties of *Capsicum chinense*, they are fiery hot. However, plant breeders can tinker with *C. chinense* peppers' heat until they taste as sweet as Bells. Even in nature, an occasional nonpungent mutant will occur; its offspring may be sweet, too. Mexican chile writers call such mutants Chile Loco—"Crazy Chile."

Taking out a syringe, Collins drew off the liquid and injected it into the HPLC machine, which consists of half a dozen metal boxes. With her finger, she traced the path of the liquid along the tubes and wires that connect one part of the machine to the other. "The liquid runs continuously through here," she said. "The molecules get excited, and detectors look at what's there."

After thirty minutes, the computer printed a graph that resembled elongated mountain peaks between desert plains on some faraway planet.

I took the printout upstairs to Bosland.

He sat in a cubicle filled with the usual professorial books and papers. Boxes on the floor overflowed with bags of commercial chile powder, tubes of medicinal ointments made from capsaicinoids, canned chiles, dried chiles, chile candy, chile-laced peanuts, and more.

He made a space for me and tapped the papers on his desk. "I'm writing an article for a European journal on breeding for quality in chiles. It sounds easy, but right away you run into trouble because first you have to define quality in a pepper, and that's definitely something else people don't agree on."

He looked at the HPLC machine's graph. "This capsaicinoid here is capsaicin," he said, pointing to one of the peaks. "And that one there is dihydrocapsaicin. The graph profiles one of a certain yellow wax type of chiles known as Santa Fe Grandes."

Why does the profile matter? I wondered.

"Because each compound affects your mouth differently."

Any given pepper contains a complex combination of capsaicinoids, but in a 1988 study, University of Georgia researchers Anna M. Krajewska and John J. Powers isolated individual capsaicinoids and asked trained volunteers who sampled very weak concentrations to describe the sensations each one created. Each capsaicinoid, it turned out, had its own characteristics. Two caused a mellow, warming effect. Some stung instantly and dissipated rapidly, while others built slowly and took a long time to fade. Some affected the front of the mouth, others the back of the tongue. Some had a fruity, spicy quality. The most irritating was homodihydrocapsaicin. Unlike other capsaicinoids, it had a noticeable aroma (testers described it as "smelling like a chile"), and it tasted sour. Both capsaicin and dihydrocapsaicin, the peaks I was staring at on the graph, created a sharp burn in the middle and back of the mouth. I was seeing scientific proof of why certain yellow peppers, which are often called Güeros (pronounced, roughly, "wear-o's") or Güeritos, taste so hot.

Or, rather, I was seeing proof for one single pepper pod.

"The thing to remember," Bosland explained, "is that with HPLC you get a very precise reading, but that precision is valid for only that one single specimen you're testing. When we start looking at, say, Jalapeños in general, or Cayennes, or New Mexico 6–4s, we're back to talking in approximations, averages, and relative terms again."

That brought us back to the question of which is the hottest pepper on earth. "You wouldn't believe how many people have sent me peppers to test," Bosland said. "It's as if everybody out there wanted to prove 'Mine's hotter than yours.'" He has tested peppers from Africa, Southeast Asia, South America, Japan, the Philippines, and just about everywhere else, including Russia. And even though no two chiles ever test out exactly alike, one variety shows up as the hottest again and again. "HPLC has finally cleared up the mystery of which is the hottest pepper on earth. It's the Habanero from the Yucatan Peninsula, a *Capsicum chinense*."

He chuckled. "I say that, and right away, someone leaps up and swears that the Scotch Bonnet is hotter. Then someone else—one of the lumpers—jumps up and says the Habanero and the Scotch Bonnet are all the same pepper. They are, and they aren't. One grows mainly in the Yucatan and the other grows mainly in the islands of the Caribbean, so we call them different land races because they grow in different places. Some people consider them different pod types, too. But the point is that it's only the orange-fruited

Habanero from the Yucatan that consistently tests hottest. Not the Scotch Bonnet. Not Habaneros from California or Texas."

In real life, peppers don't come with capsaicinoids separated into neat categories, or with pungency at just the proper low threshold to distinguish the reaction of the front of the mouth from the back. When Chileheads fall in love with a particular pepper, it's an intuitive thing, the result of the interaction of the complexity of the individual person with the complexity of the individual pepper. Just because you know the HPLC machine shows one pepper to be more potent than the next probably won't change how you'll perceive it when you eat it.

Paul Bosland understands that. And he appears content to think that even the HPLC machine is just another box that people try, unsuccessfully, to define chiles with.

In the meantime, *Chile Pepper* magazine's Dave DeWitt has seen more HPLC profiles than the average Chilehead. He knows perfectly well that the Habanero I am eating with such stoicism, as my face shifts from pink to white to red and back to white again, is verifiably hotter than his puny little green Jalapeño.

But if I asked, he'd probably wipe the bald spot on his head, which, he swears, sweats when he eats a chile that's too hot. (As Chileheads love to point out, that's called gustatory sweating.) Then he'd announce firmly, "Mine's hotter than yours."

Left: In English we associate the term *paprika* with mild chile powders from Hungary. Hungarians use the word to refer to hot peppers and powders, as well as mild. Although Spain exports twice as much paprika powder as Hungary, Hungary remains home to the largest collection of Paprika pepper folklore. According to Magyar tradition, you can measure the passion of a woman by observing how hot she likes her Paprikas. Some horticulturists call the nonpungent peppers shown here Paprika peppers. Others call them Pimientos.

Overleaf: Chileheads tell stories of peppers so hot, they can come to a boil on a cold stove. But picking the hottest pepper out of a photograph can be harder than finding Waldo. Possible winners in this photo would be the chiles with black seeds, a giveaway to their status as *Capsicum pubescens*. In Central and South America, *pubescens* chiles go by such names as the Hottest of the Hot, Kill-a-Gringo, and Raise-the-Dead chile. However, chemical tests prove Habaneros hotter. If the Habanero in the lower left was grown on the Yucatan Peninsula, it would probably beat out the black-seeded *pubescens*.

Above: When chile breeder Paul Bosland developed this ornamental *Capsicum annuum* in 1988, he named it NuMex Centennial in honor of New Mexico State University's one hundredth anniversary. (NuMex is the designation for chiles developed at New Mexico State University.) Since then seed companies and pepper growers have assigned the plant new names like Firecracker and Amethyst, but to its creator, the pepper remains NuMex Centennial. Those who try to classify peppers into pod types sometimes call this a Piquín pod type, but horticulturists argue that the conical shape of the berry removes it from that category.

Left: Chile scholars like Paul Smith believe people domesticated chiles first in the regions that show the greatest diversity of cultivated peppers today. From that Smith deduces that chiles were probably cultivated independently in different areas. Thousands of years ago, early farmers in or near Bolivia planted *Capsicum chinense, Capsicum baccatum,* and *Capsicum pubescens.* Meanwhile, in Mexico and Central America, people cultivated *Capsicum annuum* and *Capsicum frutescens.* In the arrangement shown here, the tiniest peppers are wild; others are domesticated forms of *Capsicum annuum.*

Overleaf: No one knows how many species of chiles remain to be discovered and classified. Russian collectors recently claimed to have found a new species of domesticated *Capsicum.* That is unlikely, say horticulturists, but chile experts know of at least three more wild chiles waiting to be described and named. Two will soon be formally christened. The third is more troublesome: The seeds have passed through so many hands that botanists don't know where they originated. Until the origin is known, protocol prevents scientists from naming the species. For now the nameless chiles might be christened *Capsicum mysterium* or Chile Sin Nombre.

ε   ε   ε

"Speaking for myself, I would rather live on chile and tortillas and work in a sweatshop than continue with things as they are now."

—FRANCISCO ROCHE, AUGUST 12, 1768

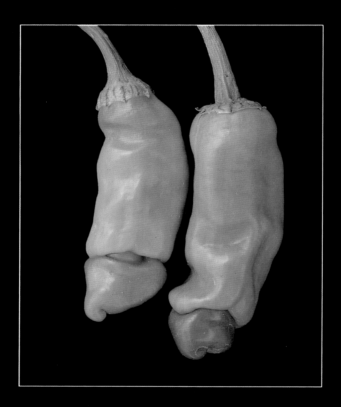

Because Peter peppers are primarily a novelty chile, scientists have not tested them for piquancy on the HPLC machine. Chileheads who move beyond gawking and joking to eating Peter peppers report that they range from mild to extremely hot.

THE PICK-YOUR-OWN-
ADVENTURE PLANT:
A History of Chiles

 IN THE AUTUMN OF 1519, HERNÁN CORTÉS AND SEVERAL HUNDRED
Spanish soldiers marched through Mexico on their way to meet Aztec emperor Montezuma
in Mexico City. Many of the Indian tribes along the way greeted them as saviors. However,
in the city of Cholula, residents welcomed the helmeted outsiders, then secretly dug pits in
which to trap them. When Cortés discovered the plot, he called city leaders in and con-
fronted them.

"We know you plan to kill us and eat us," he announced. "We know you already have the
pots boiling, and have seasoned the water with salt, ají, and tomatoes." Then the Spanish
attacked the Indians, and the chile-seasoned water presumably boiled away.

Like a stone skipping across water, chile peppers bounce in and out of the letters, diaries,
reports, first-person accounts, legends, and archaeological digs that become the basis for
history.

We know little about the centuries before and after human beings took their first fiery
bites of wild chiles roughly ten thousand years ago. By about 7000 B.C., the people of central
Mexico were eating *Capsicum annuum* chiles. Eventually they began watering and tilling the
ground around the leafy plants. Then they began saving seeds and planting chiles as a crop.
By about 4000 B.C., farmers in the Tehuacán Valley in Mexico grew chiles that, archaeolo-
gists say, looked just like those that farmers sell in markets in Mexico today.

However, no one knows when chiles or other crops were first domesticated. Chile historian Janet Long-Solís, an anthropologist at the Universidad Nacional Autónoma de México,
discusses the possibilities in her 1986 book *Capsicum y Cultura: La Historia del Chilli*.

One day recently I called Long-Solís in Mexico City, and after we'd talked awhile, she
summed up the latest anthropological theories this way: "The domestication of chile pre-
cedes that of corn and probably squash. With so little evidence available, it's ridiculous to be

This chile field in the upper Río Grande valley lies close to the site where the first colonists in New Mexico planted their first chile crops, probably in the spring of 1599. Today area farmers wait until early May to plant. If the ground is too cool, the chile seeds won't germinate, and another round of seeds must be pushed into the earth.

too precise. But we now believe that chiles were probably among the first crops domesticated in the New World, along with beans and avocados."

We don't know why ancient farmers focused on peppers so early. Perhaps they first cultivated those fruits and vegetables that they considered most valuable. If so, they prized chiles highly.

In South America, Peruvians and Bolivians became the continent's champion chile fans. In some versions of the Inca origin myths, the brothers of Manco Cápac, founder of the Incan empire, were named Cachi, Uchu, and Sauca: Salt, Chile, and Satisfaction.

By 1400 A.D., cultivated and wild chiles grew from what is now southern Texas all the way down to northern Argentina, but they remained strictly in the Western Hemisphere. It's hard to believe that a food staple as fundamental to the cuisines of Africa, India, Indonesia, China, Hungary, and other parts of the world would have arrived so late in all those places. But scholars can find no linguistic, archaeo-logical, artistic, or botanical proof that chiles had spread anywhere beyond the Americas before 1492. That doesn't mean eaters lacked curries in India or spicy foods in parts of China, pepper authority Barbara Pickersgill points out. It just means they used other spices, such as ginger and pungent relatives of cardamom.

When Columbus sailed westward, he hoped to discover an easier way to obtain black pepper (*Piper nigrum*), the most highly prized spice of his day. Reaching the Caribbean Islands, Columbus and his shipmates watched the natives seasoning their meat with tiny, pungent chiles.

On January 15, 1493, he wrote in his diary that the islanders ate "much ají, which is their pepper, of a kind more valuable than black pepper, and nobody eats without it, because they find it so healthful." We don't know how Columbus reacted to his own first bite of ají. But apparently he liked it, because he suggested that the Spanish could load fifty ships full of chiles every year in Hispaniola.

When Columbus returned from his first voyage, he

brought peppers with him to Spain. With that, Capsicums began circling the world. Scholars do not agree on the details of how peppers arrived in places like Africa, India, Hungary, and China. However, Jean Andrews, a pepper expert in Austin, Texas, has searched through early reports and determined that, one way or another, chile peppers had arrived in all those places within one hundred years of Columbus's voyages. Still, as Ping-Ti Ho, a professor at Canada's University of British Columbia, pointed out in 1955, "It is foolish to believe that a certain plant can be introduced into a new area only once, and then only by a certain route."

Meanwhile, back in the Americas, Spanish newcomers found the peoples of Central and South America devouring chiles in quantities that are hard to imagine today. Francisco Bernardino de Sahagún translated Nahuatl accounts of Aztec daily life. Vendors at the marketplace in Mexico City sold "hot chiles, chiles from Atzitziuacan, small chiles, chile powder, yellow chile, chile from the Couixca, sharp-pointed red chiles, long chiles, and smoked chiles."

In a chapter that begins, "Here are told the foods which the lords ate," Sahagún listed dishes made from peppers. Chefs served Aztec aristocrats turkey with yellow chiles and turkey with green chiles. They made a meat stew, similar to posole, that included corn and red chiles. They cooked meat in a sauce of red chiles, tomatoes, and ground squash seeds. That same vegetable trio livened lobster dishes and meals of sardines. Cooks prepared salsas from tomatoes and yellow chiles, and tomatoes and green chiles. They served white fish with yellow chiles, and gray fish with red chiles. They prepared frog with green chiles, newt with yellow chiles, and tadpole with small chiles. They made a thick meatless soup from yellow chiles. They used dried chiles to season purslane sauces and amaranth greens.

One of Cortés's companions, Bernal Díaz del Castillo, said that even Montezuma, who at every meal could choose among more dishes and foods than most people have ever seen, ate "a slight breakfast, not of meats, but vegetables, such as ají."

One final detail confirms the importance these early Mexicans placed on peppers. When they wished to appease the gods, they gave up two of their greatest pleasures: chile peppers and making love.

Farther north, in what is today the U.S. Southwest, archaeological, ethnobotanical, and other evidence suggests that the Anasazi Indians never learned to enjoy the tiny wild Chiltepíns and other peppers which must have reached them along the ancient trade routes. When Spanish explorers under Antonio Espejo traveled to what is now New Mexico and Arizona in 1582–83, they noticed this culinary lack. Wrote one of the expedition's chroniclers, Baltasar Obregón, "They have no chile, but the natives were given some seed to plant."

Apparently, the Pueblos accepted the gift politely and set the seeds aside. Then in 1598, Spanish colonists arrived in northern New Mexico, bringing with them an acquired taste for chile peppers. In 1601, one of the colonists, Francisco de Valverde, listed the crops the Pueblo Indians grew; chile was still not among them.

But the Spanish colonists planted both hot chiles and milder peppers. Complained Valverde, "The mice eat the chile and peppers so fast that if the latter are not harvested in time, the mice do not leave anything."

By the time of the Pueblo Revolt of 1680, the Pueblo Indians apparently had acquired a taste for peppers. After driving the Spanish out of New Mexico, Indian leaders tried to purge themselves of all Spanish influences. An Indian named Juan from Tesuque Pueblo, north of Santa Fe, reported in 1681 that Indian leaders even ordered their people "to burn the seeds which the Spaniards sowed and to plant only corn and beans, which were the crops of their ancestors."

Juan confessed that some people disobeyed and sowed the Spanish seeds anyway. They did this, he explained, "because of their fondness for the Spaniards." Maybe. Or maybe it was their fondness for chiles.

People's use of peppers and reactions to them over the past five centuries would fill an encyclopedia. Jean Andrews has collected some of the liveliest historical comments in her classic book *Peppers: The Domesticated Capsicums*. Thanks to Andrews, Chileheads everywhere have chuckled over such pronouncements as this 1595 observation by Flemish physician Rembert Dodoens: "It killeth dogs, if it be given them to eat." Or sixteenth-century cartographer José de Acosta's warning, "The use thereof is prejudiciall to the health of young folkes, chiefly to the soule, for that it provokes to lust." Perhaps best known of all is Francisco Ximénez's 1722 observation about a chile from Havana, probably a *Capsicum chinense*, so strong it could make "a bull unable to eat."

But even Andrews couldn't catalog all the reports of chiles in the New World in the centuries after Columbus. Hidden in diaries, letters, and official documents from the 1600s, 1700s, and 1800s, many references hint at the early spread of peppers in what is now the United States.

On December 2, 1621, the governor of Bermuda wrote

Left: Over the centuries, the chiles the Spanish colonists brought to New Mexico from Mexico developed into distinct land races—varieties of peppers associated with a specific locale. In northern New Mexico, land races that survive include Chimayó, Española, Dixon, San Juan, and Velarde chiles. These land races tend to have thinner walls—and therefore less flesh—than standard New Mexico chiles. But they taste better, too, say their proponents. Here, baskets of Velarde and Española chiles sit waiting to be roasted the traditional way in an adobe *horno* (oven) at Orlando Casados, Jr.'s farm along the upper Río Grande.

Below: Before dawn farm workers stack aspenwood inside the *horno*. Once it has burned to coals, they begin roasting the chiles. In about ten minutes the skins blacken and loosen. Visitors from as far away as India and Thailand have come to observe Casados's traditional farming methods, which include a centuries-old irrigation system known as *acequias*.

that he was sending red chiles to the governor of Virginia. In an expedition diary entry for January 12, 1719, Fray Francisco Céliz reported that the new governor of Texas, Martín de Alarcón, had ordered chile seeds brought in for planting. French naval officer Jean-Bernard Bossu, who traveled extensively in what is now the United States between 1751 and 1762, reported that during the two months he spent with the Indians of Alabama, he lived on native dishes made from dried or smoked game, which was roasted or boiled. "This food, called chili, is very tasty and healthful," he observed.

Among all these accounts, my own favorites include those by two German-speaking Jesuit priests who lived in Sonora (what is now southern Arizona and northern Sonora, Mexico) in the 1700s.

Like many Europeans of his day, Swiss-born Philipp Segesser, who moved to southern Arizona in 1732, called chiles "Turkish pepper." He wrote, "This kind of pepper, which we grow as a decorative plant in Luzern gardens, is very much used in this country, where it serves in place of real pepper." Spanish colonists, he said, "prize no food higher than that which is spiced with Turkish pepper. It bites the tongue mightily."

In a 1737 report, Segesser included a recipe for chili stew. "The red fruit is placed on glowing coals until it is easily ground up. The grinding or crushing is done in a mortar or on a stone, while water is occasionally poured upon it. The ground-up pepper is then dumped into hot lard and cooked with pieces of meat."

Sounds delicious. But Segesser didn't think so. He concluded his recipe by saying, "Turkish pepper is too hot for me; I burned my tongue upon it only once."

Two decades later, another German-speaking Jesuit, Ignaz Pfefferkorn, who was born near Cologne, arrived in Sonora. He found Spanish colonists harvesting wild peppers and growing their own. "Even when the fruit is not yet ripe, the Spaniards' mouths water for it," he wrote. "They eat it with such appetite that their mouths froth and tears come to their eyes. They are fonder of this food than we are of the finest garden lettuce." The colonists pickled chiles in vinegar, strung them into long strands called ristras to dry, mixed them with meat, and cooked them into what Pfefferkorn called "the universal sauce."

To make this sauce, which was another early variant of chili stew, they removed and discarded the seeds and ribs of the chiles, added water to what was left, and crushed it with a grinding stone. Then they put the bits of chiles through a

There are almost as many methods for making ristras as there are ristra makers. One way is to tie chile pods together in clusters at three-inch intervals along a cotton string. Then wrap the clusters around a baling wire or heavy twine. Here, a young woman ties red chiles together at El Rancho de las Golondrinas, a museum of living history on the outskirts of Santa Fe, New Mexico. Most ristras sold throughout the United States come from New Mexico, where the arid air allows the chiles to dry quickly without rotting, molding, or attracting insects.

In the linguistic comedy that could be titled "Chile Pepper Names," some peppers take on new appellations when they dry. Other name changes relate to geography. In Indiana, Illinois, southwestern Ohio, and Kentucky, people have called Bell peppers Mangoes for so long that even Webster's dictionary recognizes that usage. Ohio chile expert Hardy Eshbaugh has tried for thirty years to trace the origin of this misnomer, but hasn't been able to confirm any of the numerous possibilities. *Chile Pepper* magazine editor Dave DeWitt suggests the mixup began decades ago when a group of immigrant workers who missed the real mangoes in their homeland substituted Bell peppers in recipes that called for mangoes.

sieve, fried them in a pan with fat and previously cooked meat, and boiled the results "for some time." Colonists ate this sauce every day of the year and poured it on dishes ranging from boiled fish to baked eggs. "The constant use of this hot sauce is at first an unbelievable hardship for the European," Pfefferkorn reported. Then he launched into his own first-time-I-tried-it anecdote.

The priest had just finished a fifteen-hour journey. He was exhausted. He was starved. And his only choices were a piece of dry bread—or this ubiquitous sauce. He chose the sauce. "After the first mouthful the tears started to come," he wrote. "I could not say a word and believed I had hell-fire in my mouth."

Unlike Segesser, Pfefferkorn tried again. "One becomes accustomed to it after frequent bold victories," he wrote, "so that with time the dish becomes tolerable and finally agreeable."

Wild chiles, the same Chiltepíns that grow in southern Arizona and Texas today, were even hotter, Pfefferkorn said. But Spanish colonists devoured them, too. The cook would place whole Chiltepíns in a salt cellar on the table. Diners helped themselves to as many of the caustic round berries as they thought they could eat. They squashed the Chiltepíns with their fingers and mixed the results directly into their food. Pfefferkorn said the Spanish colonists "swear that it is exceedingly healthful and very good as an aid to the digestion."

Seven decades later, after Mexico gained independence from Spain, Americans began traveling down the Santa Fe Trail. In his 1844 book *Commerce of the Prairies,* Josiah Gregg reported that chiles, beans, and atole (a drink made from ground corn) were the three staples of New Mexican cuisine. Hispanic New Mexicans ate red or green chiles with every meal. The Pueblo Indians ate so many peppers that Gregg decided the Spanish colonists of New Mexico had learned to eat them from the Pueblos.

The California gold rush of 1849 introduced thousands of Americans to chile peppers and chili stew. Vermont-born William Lewis Manly's comments were typical. After nearly dying of hunger in Death Valley in the winter of 1849–1850, he and his friends continued westward until they encountered some Hispanic settlers who fed them a multicourse meal. "Everything is new and strange to us," Manly reported. After an initial round of tortillas (which Manly called "some kind of slapjacks"), their hosts served baked squash and beans seasoned with chiles. "Then came a dish of dried meat pounded fine, mixed with green peppers [chiles] and well

Above: In southern Texas, southern Arizona, and northern Mexico, the Chiltepín, a wild variety of *Capsicum annuum,* still grows among the desert vegetation. In southern Arizona, the town of Tumacacori received its name from an archaic O'odham Indian word meaning "pepper bush" or "place where Chiltepíns grow." Native Seeds/SEARCH of Tucson is working to establish Chiltepín reserves.

Left: In 1868 Edmund McIlhenny of New Orleans, Louisiana, began bottling a zingy new pepper sauce that he called Tabasco. The sauce's bite was reportedly so strong it diverted people from their unhappy memories of the Civil War and gave them something to laugh about. Since then, Tabasco sauce has become the best-known pepper sauce in the world.

PIQUANCY: TWO PEPPERS

SNAPPY OATMEAL COOKIES

4 dried Chiles de Arbol
1/2 cup milk
1 egg
1/4 cup canola oil
1/3 cup plain (unsweetened) nonfat yoghurt
1/2 cup brown sugar
1 teaspoon vanilla
1½ cups flour
1/2 teaspoon salt
1/2 teaspoon baking soda
1½ cups uncooked oats
1 cup chopped walnuts
3/4 cup raisins

Wearing rubber gloves, remove and discard the stems from the Chiles de Arbol. Break the chiles into small pieces and place in a one-quart saucepan. Add the milk and cook over low heat. Remove from heat just before milk starts to boil. Cool mixture and whip in a blender until the Chiles de Arbol are pulverized. Add egg, oil, yoghurt, brown sugar, and vanilla, and whip another minute. Set aside.

Combine flour, salt, and baking soda, and stir well. Add the wet mixture and stir until well blended. Mix in oats. Add walnuts and raisins and continue to stir until oats, walnuts, and raisins are uniformly distributed throughout.

Bake on a greased cookie sheet at 350 degrees for about fifteen minutes or until cookies are light brown.

---

fried in beef tallow. This seemed to be the favorite dish of the proprietors, but was a little too hot for our people. They called it *chili cum carne*—meat with pepper—and we soon found this to be one of the best dishes cooked by the Californians."

In pre– and post–Civil War Louisiana, people experimented with various *Capsicum frutescens* and *C. annuum* chiles, including the wild Chiltepín, in hopes of creating the perfect pepper sauce. No two accounts of what happened next agree. But this much is certain: In 1868 a bearded banker named Edmund McIlhenny started what has become the most famous chile business in the world, the McIlhenny Company, makers of the trademarked Tabasco brand pepper sauce. In the United States since then, probably more people have tasted capsaicinoids first through McIlhenny's Tabasco Sauce than by any other means.

Meanwhile, chiles had become so established in India and the Orient that people imagined they had originated there. European diners, though, remained more cautious. During the 1600s and 1700s most Capsicums except nonpungent Bell peppers remained primarily an ornamental plant and a source of pranks. But not in Hungary. There, pining for spices that only the wealthy could afford, peasants began eating both mild and hot peppers, which they called Paprikas. As the generations passed, Hungarian housewives learned to pickle green chiles in vinegar and serve them with boiled or fried meat. They ground ripe red chiles into powders, which they added to goulash. Like Spanish colo-

nists in Arizona, New Mexico, and other parts of the New World, they braided red chiles into ristras to dry for later use.

In the late 1700s, Hungarian aristocrats finally noticed that the foods the peasants ate tasted better then theirs. Barons and countesses switched to peasant fare. After that, visitors from other countries who dined with the aristocrats began associating Hungarian cuisine with chile powders. Hungarians themselves ate a full range of peppers and pepper powders, from hot to mild. But beyond Hungary, the mildest of their powders became known as Hungarian paprika, or simply paprika.

Since then, chile powders, and especially powders of the hotter chiles, have become the most heavily used spice on earth, and an estimated 75 percent of the world's population eats chiles as a basic part of their diet. In Africa, Ethiopians make a hot sauce so scorching that one cup requires fourteen dried Chile Piquíns and a tablespoon of powdered Cayenne. Indonesian cooks crush Cayennes into explosive sambal sauces. Chile-spiced eel has become a delicacy in southern Spain. Vodka now comes laced with chile peppers. In France, a single importer in 1991 sold French cooks twenty-one tons of fresh Jalapeños, two tons of Chipotles (dried, smoked Jalapeños), six tons of chile powder, and three tons of dried chiles.

Overall, North Americans waited a long time before succumbing to incendiary foods. True, regional cooking in places like Texas, California, New Mexico, and Arizona zapped culinary thrillseekers' tastebuds and tongues. Louisi-

Tabasco peppers, a variety of *Capsicum frutescens*, rate high on anyone's heat scale. The McIlhennys still grow Tabascos on Avery Island, Louisiana, to harvest for seed, but farmers in Latin America grow most of the Tabasco peppers that go into McIlhenny's famous sauce. According to folk history, the name of Baton Rouge, Louisiana, came from the red stick that farmers still use to test the color of ripened Tabascos. Unless a pepper is as red as the stick, it isn't red enough. Linguists link the name of the pepper to the state of Tabasco, Mexico, but the McIlhenny family believes the pepper received its name from their trademarked sauce.

ana chefs used chiles in gumbo and other dishes. Mexican restaurants as far north as Alaska served enchiladas so *picoso* that diners cried between bites. Cooks in Cincinnati, Ohio, poured chile sauce on spaghetti, and diners in Buffalo, New York, smothered chicken wings in hot sauce. But for decades, the general public consensus seemed to be that there was something suspicious or low class about people who enjoyed jolting their senses with capsaicinoids.

I remember visiting British Columbia frequently with my family in the early 1960s. We always ate at an inexpensive Chinese restaurant where the owner cautioned non-Asians to avoid the hot and spicy dishes. He knew that most mainstream North Americans remained willing to try chiles in minute amounts, but were always ready to end the relationship at the first hint of serious heat.

Then something happened. By the 1980s more and more North American diners found they liked to keep their tastebuds guessing with chile flavors that ranged from sweet to hell-fire hot. Thai, East Indian, and Szechuan restaurants opened in cities across the continent. In some sections of the beach communities of Los Angeles, you could find one in every block for miles on end. When I returned to Vancouver, B.C., in 1986, I ate at East Indian, Chinese, and Southeast Asian restaurants where waiters encouraged diners to try the hottest foods they could stand.

Meanwhile, ketchup had remained the number one condiment in the United States for decades. As our parents had done before us, we splashed ketchup on hamburgers, poured it on French fries, added it to meatloaf. But sometime during the 1980s, all those squashed tomatoes began to taste bland. More and more, as we pushed our shopping carts down grocery store aisles, we passed up the ketchup and picked up a jar of mouth-jangling chile salsa.

If what we eat defines who we are, as food writers say, then in 1991 the average American officially became a different person. That year chile-laced salsas bumped ketchup the king of condiments off the throne, as Americans spent $640 million on salsas and only $600 million on ketchup.

At the same time, fresh chiles and other chile-based items reached store shelves in every U.S. state and Canadian province. Shoppers at farmers' markets as far north as Quebec could buy chiles grown by local farmers. It was all part of what writer Raymond Sokolov has called "the largest revolution in eating habits since Columbus brought the two hemispheres together." On the eve of the five-hundredth anniversary of Columbus's arrival in the Americas, North Americans had finally begun eating like true citizens of the Americas.

Generations of Arkansas housewives have raised peppers in their gardens. Rosa Bruch, who grew up in the early 1900s in Bleeker, recalls the blistering Rose pepper, which resembled a small rosebud and made all other peppers seem tame. Even as a preschooler, her son Forrest would pick Rose peppers and eat them like candy. "He'd cry between bites, but then he'd go back for more." Frances Mitchell of Sheridan, Arkansas, canned the peppers shown here, which go locally by the name Hot Peppers. In appearance and pungency they resemble several varieties of hot Mexican and Asian peppers.

ELECTRIC BLANKETS

10 slices of uncooked top round beef, 1/8 inch thick and
    approximately 3–4 inches wide and 4–5 inches long
10 canned whole green New Mexico (Anaheim) chiles
salt and coarse-grind black pepper
3 ounces grated Parmesan cheese
2 medium onions, chopped fine
2 red Bell peppers, chopped fine
3–4 Tablespoons olive or canola oil
1 bunch fresh spinach
3 ounces pine nuts, chopped extra fine
2 teaspoons chopped cilantro leaves
a grating of fresh nutmeg
approximately 3 cups water

Pound the meat to tenderize. Spread each strip out flat on a chopping board or other work area. Salt and pepper each piece lightly. Wearing rubber gloves, drain the green chiles, cut them open lengthwise, and pat them dry with paper towels; spread one chile out flat across a piece of meat, covering completely; repeat for each piece of meat. Sprinkle two-thirds of each piece of chile-covered meat with grated Parmesan cheese, leaving the top third bare.

Place the oil in a stainless steel skillet and cook the onions and red Bell peppers, covered over low heat, for about forty-five minutes, stirring frequently. Meanwhile, wash the spinach well and cook it over low heat in a covered kettle until it turns limp and flat (five to ten minutes). Allow it to cool, then drain and reserve any excess liquid and chop the spinach well. When the onion and Bell pepper mixture has finished cooking, add the spinach, pine nuts, cilantro, and nutmeg. Mix well.

Place about two tablespoons of this mixture in a neat line at the Parmesan-covered end of the meat strips. Roll the meat forward around this mixture. Pack the meat rolls together tightly down the center of a 13x9x2-inch glass baking pan. Pour any remaining spinach water into the bottom of the pan and add enough additional water to reach just below the tops of the rolls. Place any remaining vegetable mixture along the top of the rolls, centering it down the middle of the row.

Cover the pan tightly with aluminum foil and bake in the oven at 325 degrees for about two hours. The water turns into a rich broth and can be used in place of gravy. Serve the Electric Blankets with baked, mashed, or dauphine potatoes. Serves four.

For hotter blankets, add one or two Jalapeños, chopped extra fine, to the onion mixture after it is cooked.

Within one hundred years of Columbus's explorations, chile peppers reached Asia, Africa, and Europe. Pepper experts theorize that the first species to travel were *Capsicum annuum* and *Capsicum frutescens. Capsicum baccatum,* a South American species, probably didn't reach the Old World until the twentieth century. Outside botanical gardens, *Capsicum pubescens* still grows almost exclusively in the Americas. Just looking at the peppers shown here, even experts can't identify them by species, but they're probably *C. baccatum* or *C. annuum.* Because of their shape, they are definitely not *C. pubescens,* in spite of their hairy stems.

Above: Nonpungent *annuums* like these Red Ruffled peppers (also called Tomato peppers) have been popular in Europe for centuries. On his way to the Americas in 1754, Würzburg native Joseph Och stopped in Alicante, Spain, where he found people eating melons for breakfast. "Should one chill his stomach through eating them," he wrote, "he may help the matter with some Pimentones or Spanish peppers, larger than a fist and, according to what is said of them, very sweet." Vendors in the marketplace had so many sweet peppers for sale that they stacked them six feet high.

Right: When Europeans first arrived in Mexico, they found Mexicans eating chiles for breakfast. Some still do. In the nonfiction book *Son of Tecúnumán*, a Mayan Indian writes in a diary entry for February 1973, "After bathing early in the lake, I ate fish broth with lots of chili for breakfast." Here, vendors at the Mercado Central in Acapulco, Mexico, sell two ancient crops of the Americas side by side: chiles and tobacco.

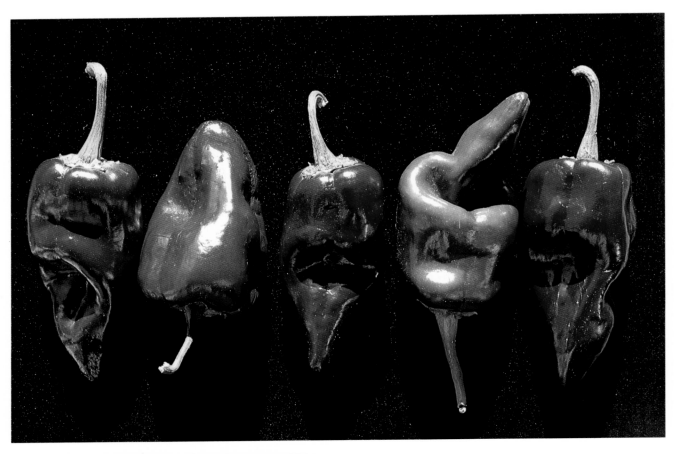

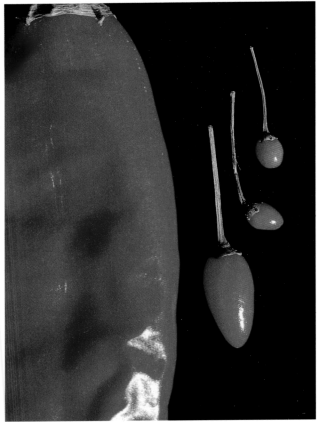

Above: These mild *Capsicum annuum* peppers are often called Poblanos when fresh, Anchos when dry. Varieties of Poblano that turn darker become known as Mulatos or Chile de Chocolate when dried. However, grocery stores, farm workers, and others often ignore these distinctions and shift names around as lightly as chile plants shift their genes. Some vendors even label these chiles Pasillas. If they're not too dizzy when they step off this linguistic merry-go-round, people use fresh Poblanos to make king-size chiles rellenos and dried ones to make sauces and stews.

Left: Peppers range from more than a foot long to less than a quarter inch. Often larger peppers taste milder, and smaller peppers hotter. But chile aficionados approach any unknown pepper—and even many known peppers—with caution. Two lookalike chiles may contain numbingly different concentrations of capsaicinoids.

Above: During a seven-day battle for control of Mexico City in 1521, Spanish soldiers fought all day and stayed awake all night watching for the enemy. Wrote one of the soldiers, Bernal Díaz del Castillo, "In the evening we retired to console ourselves with our misery of corn cakes, chiles, prickly pear cactus, and herbs." Meanwhile Montezuma reportedly fretted to his advisors, "I feel as if I were drowning in chiles." Montezuma and his subjects ate dozens of varieties of *Capsicum annuum* chiles, some of which resembled the hot peppers shown above.

Right: Italians name this mild pepper Corno di Toro—Bull's Horn—because of its shape. Italian cookbooks suggest slicing the thin-walled peppers, which are a variety of *Capsicum annuum,* into salads or sautéing them with tomatoes and garlic. Those who categorize chiles into pod types sometimes call these Cuban chiles; others link them to New Mexico chiles.

ک ک ک

"One bowl of your chili would pollute the waters of the Great Salt Lake."
—H. ALLEN SMITH, 1967

Carroll Shelby remembers the days when a full-sized chili cookoff consisted of three contestants. Now a small cookoff draws twenty cooks or more. A founding member of the International Chili Society, Shelby knows just how vile someone else's chili can taste. His own chili tastes—well, judge for yourself: For every two pounds of beef, he pours in one can of beer. Along with the usual spices and chile powders, he stirs three-quarters of a pound of grated goat cheese into the pot half an hour before it's finished. Here, he tastes someone else's chili.

"VILE SLOP":
Chili Stew and Other Foods

ONE NOVEMBER DAY, WHEN OTHER VISITORS TO THE PHOENIX area golfed, wandered among saguaro cactus, and relaxed under the blue Arizona sky, ninety-three chefs cooked chili stew in makeshift kitchens in a dusty lot at Rawhide on the north end of Scottsdale. Some chopped fresh green chiles, or measured dark red chile powder in the palms of their hands. Others seared beef, pork, or lamb in kettles over propane burners. Some lined their remaining ingredients up in the order in which they needed them: garlic, onion, salt, black pepper. Others studied the handwritten recipes they had created while cooking hundreds of pots of chili stew. Most of the chefs appeared to have a nervous feeling in their stomachs. They'd arrived at a moment they'd cooked towards and thought about for months or even years: the World's Championship Chili Cookoff, sponsored by the International Chili Society (ICS).

All ninety-three contestants had battled chili cooks elsewhere to gain a table here. Charlie and Barbara Ward of Lake Havasu City, Arizona, traveled with chili pots and chopping knives across the country for months until Barbara won the Massachusetts State Championship and Charlie won the Gulf Coast Regional Championship; the year before that, they cooked their way to first place in New Mexico and Tennessee. Ed Pierczynski, 56, a second-generation Polish-American and family-practice physician from Carson City, Nevada, stirred his way northward with pot after pot of chili until he reached Vancouver, British Columbia, where he won the Canadian Championship. Warren Chan, a chef from Calgary, Alberta, who has made it to the world cookoff six times, carried his recipe westward over the mountains to win the British Columbia Regionals. Michael Kroeker of Manitoba fought off outsiders at the Manitoba Regional contest for the right to represent his home province.

Now musicians played country and western music on the portastage, and an estimated twenty thousand visitors picked up samples from some of the cookoff's sponsors: miniature

Al Rock of Fremont, California, wears this United States Chili Marshal badge to cookoffs across the country. "I'm looking for chili abuse," he drawls. Chili abuse is chili lover's code for "chili made a way I personally don't like." Like many other chili fans, Rock lugs his pots and peppers to fifteen or more cookoffs a year. A construction foreman supervisor, he has earned as much as $5,000 in chili prizes in one year.

bottles of McIlhenny's Tabasco sauce at one booth, packets of chile powder from the American Spice Trade Association at another. Meanwhile, retired Senator Barry Goldwater's granddaughters offered samples of their Taste of the Southwest brand of salsas. But the real question was, Who would create the chili that would win $25,000 in a double-blind tasting test that involved almost as many judges as cooks?

An estimated four thousand chili cookoffs take place across North America and around the world each year. They may be as informal as two neighbors in Texas swapping bowls of chili across their backyard fences, or as formal as the ICS World Cookoff. ICS alone sanctions more than three hundred cookoffs, and approximately 700,000 people attend these annually, either as onlookers, tasters, or cooks.

A rival group, the Chili Appreciation Society International (CASI), sanctions another 480 cookoffs in the United States, Canada, and abroad, raising more than half a million dollars yearly for charities. In 1992 alone, 14,732 chili cooks battled each other in CASI cookoffs. Winners from CASI

contests meet each November in Terlingua, Texas, for a giant international cookoff that features 360 competitors.

A third group, the Original Terlingua International Championship Chili Cookoff, produces a chili extravaganza in Terlingua the same weekend. Magazines, furniture stores, shopping malls, and chambers of commerce sponsor uncounted other cookoffs. There are cookoffs in such unexpected places as Alaska, Hawaii, Maine, Germany, and even France, all focusing on one dish: chili stew, or simply chili.

The one essential ingredient in chili is chile peppers: fresh, dry, whole, chopped, or powdered; mild, medium, or blisteringly hot. Most chili lovers insist on adding some type of meat. Typically they use sirloin beef, but Texans have been known to toss in armadillo, skunk, or rattlesnake. Alaskans sometimes add salmon. Other cooks around North America claim chili tastes best when prepared with wild musk hog, raccoon, venison, buffalo, moose, beaver, goat, or opposum. Australians reportedly do them one better by adding kangaroo meat or even emu ham.

Some cooks add beans, but neither ISC nor CASI permits this controversial ingredient at its cookoffs. (A. Vann York, former president of CASI, once told me, "If you know beans about chili, you know chili has no beans.") Some insist on adding cumin, but Santa Fe history librarian Orlando Romero, who points out that his ancestors have been cooking with chile peppers for four hundred years, believes that cumin makes chili inedible. Ditto oregano and tomatoes.

As Jim West, executive director of ICS, says, "There are almost as many recipes for chili as there are chili cooks." In Idaho, a meatless chili contains lentils and potatoes. In Hawaii, hostesses serve chili with chow mein noodles and rice. In Cincinnati, home to more than 120 chili parlors, cooks guard their chili recipes more closely than some countries protect plutonium, but aficionados swear they detect cinnamon between bites of the spaghetti the chili is served on. And every chili cook, it seems, believes that his or her own personal recipe, developed after years of work, tastes better than anyone else's.

The ancestors of the Aztecs or the Incas may have been the first to argue about who made the best chili stew, but the chili cookoff, in contemporary times, originated in 1967 in Texas. That year New York humor writer H. Allen Smith, who grew up in Illinois, wrote an article for *Holiday* magazine entitled, "Nobody Knows More About Chili Than I Do." In it, he said of chili cooks, "Each of us knows that *his* chili is light years beyond other chili in quality and singularity; each of us knows that all other chili is such vile slop that a coyote would turn his back on it."

When they heard that, a group of chili lovers led by Carroll Shelby invited Smith to Terlingua, Texas, for a high-noon cookdown with an Austin, Texas, chili expert and newspaperman named Wick Fowler on the porch of the Chisos Oasis Saloon.

Not many people remember that cookoff. But Ormly Gumfudgin, 70, the official historian for ICS, does. While Warren Chan, the Wards, Ed Pierczynski, and the eighty-nine other contestants were busily stirring their chili and debating whether to stick to their recipes or throw in a little extra cumin, oregano, or chile powder just this once, I hunted

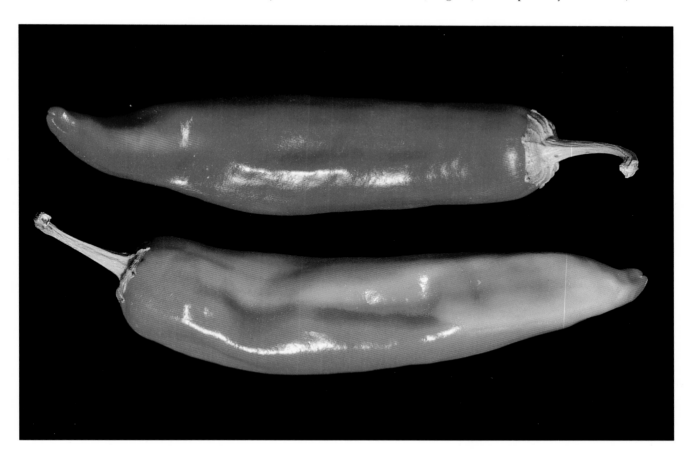

Plant breeder Roy Nakayama, son of Japanese-American truck farmers, named NuMex Big Jim in honor of a farmer friend, Jim Lytle. The long, mild pepper grows to a foot or more and has been called the longest chile on earth. It's probably not the largest, though. In overall mass, some Bells are bigger.

Ormly up. He had white hair and a yellow mustache and was wearing a pink ruffled shirt. On his hip dangled a holster that contained a bottle of Pepto Bismol, another of the cookoff's sponsors. The buttons and pins that covered his hat included one that said, "I'm so horny, even the crack of dawn looks good."

Ormly tamped the tobacco down in his corncob pipe with his finger. Then he reminisced. "Shelby called me in August of 1967 early one morning. He woke me up. It was 7:30 or something. He said, 'Hey Orm, How'd you like to go to Texas for a chili cookoff?' So I did. We had two cooks, and three judges. One judge voted for H. Allen Smith, another voted for Wick Fowler. The third judge screamed and spit his chili out onto the porch floor and claimed his taste buds had been *ruint*—spell that r-u-i-n-t. So they agreed they could not make a decision and we had to come back next year.

"So the next year we came back, and after the judging a masked bandido with a rifle jumped up onto the front porch and stole the ballot box.

"So then the third year, Shelby said, 'We better have a winner this year,' and we did: C. V. Wood, Jr. He went on to become one of the board of governors of ICS." Ormly removed his hat. "But now he's gone to the Great Chili Cookoff in the Sky."

To a lot of chili cooks, whackiness is what chili cookoffs are supposed to be all about: what the late Frank X. Tolbert, author of the 1966 classic, *A Bowl of Red*, called "enough chili and craziness to boggle the imagination." Never mind the CASI and ICS rules about ingredients, preparation time, cooking time, and so on. The point of all this stirring, chopping, cooking, and tasting is to find a happy outlet for the madness that arises from living in the late twentieth century, or maybe just from living.

Take the insult H. Allen Smith once spit at his brother Sam: "One bowl of your chili would pollute the waters of the Great Salt Lake." Stop and think a minute, and other possible putdowns may float up effortlessly through the fragrance of roasting green chiles. "One bowl of your chili would make Niagara Falls turn around and run backwards." "One bowl of your chili would kill Dracula." "One bowl of your chili . . ."

After Ormly and I finished swapping stories and insults, he went off to join the other judges, each holstered with Pepto Bismol, at four tables lined with ninety-three anonymously coded cups of chili. The top twenty-five chilis from those tables moved to the finals table, where Robert Mitchum's actor son Chris Mitchum and other tasters sampled with earnest faces and made notes on their judging pads.

Meanwhile, the waiting chefs passed the time ladling out bite-sized portions of chili to hungry onlookers. I wandered among them. "If I don't win this time, I'll be back again," said Warren Chan, as he and his wife packed his utensils away for the return trip to Alberta. Charlie Ward, who judges cookoffs when he isn't entering them, explained to tasters around his kettle that in a good chili no single flavor predominates. Michael Kroeker shared his special Manitoba chili recipe with the crowd who had emptied his kettle: "Molasses," he said. "That's one of my secrets. I add a little molasses. I use fresh green Jalapeños, celery, Bell peppers. Oh, yes, and lamb."

In the booth marked Canadian Championship, Ed Pierczynski looked as gloomy as an all-around cheerful person can. "I haven't got a chance," he said, scraping out the last bite of chili from the bottom of the pan and handing it to me.

"Tastes fantastic," I said. "Smooth. Hot, but not too spicy. Just right."

"Well, I don't know. I was trying so hard to make sure it tasted smooth that I got everything backwards. I always season it twice, once at the beginning, and once after cooking for an hour and a half. The first time, I use chile powder, garlic powder, onion powder, and Tabasco sauce. The second time I put in more chile powder, more Tabasco sauce, and cumin. Only somehow I got the two batches of spices mixed up, and put the second one in first. So then I spent three hours trying to correct my mistakes."

He shrugged. "It doesn't matter. We've had a good time. I'll go home and start cooking all over again, and if I'm lucky, next year I'll be back."

By the time the master of ceremonies finally came on stage, every kettle was empty, and all the chefs stood ready to carry their equipment away.

To shrieks and applause, the M.C. announced the winners. Three people tied for fifth place, including Charlie Ward.

In African countries like Zaire, tribal farmers jumble crops together and grow chiles among peanut and tobacco plants. They typically raise *Capsicum annuum* peppers to eat as a vegetable and *Capsicum frutescens* to grind up and use as a spice. In parts of Africa chile peppers have reverted to a wild state and are propagated like other wild peppers, through bird droppings. The African peppers shown here fall under the broad general name Pili-Pili, a Swahili word whose multiple meanings include vivid sexual references. Like South America's Ají, the term applies to any species of peppers.

Two tied for fourth, including Ohio attorney Randy Robinson, defending champ. Third place went to Seattleite Doug Wilkey, holder of the Pacific Northwest Regional title. Second place went to Oklahoman Betty Phillips, who represented Kansas. Then the physician who'd cooked his way north to Canada heard his name called: Ed Pierczynski had won first place.

"I can't believe it," he beamed, as he hoisted an oversized $25,000 check from one of the cookoff's sponsors, Hunt-Wesson, over his head. "Now I have to turn in the winning recipe, and the awful truth is, I'm not even sure what's in it."

H. Allen Smith, Wick Fowler, and Frank X. Tolbert would have been proud.

Most chile dishes don't attract the sort of attention that chili stew does. But leaf through cookbooks of the world, and you'll see that chile peppers are the exclamation points, the accent marks, and the expletives in the universal language that is food. Nobody knows for sure, but there are probably at least one million recipes, worldwide, that include chiles as an ingredient.

Among my own favorites is the garnish that accompanies such Japanese dishes as Tori No Mizutaki, a chicken and vegetable casserole, and Karei No Karaage, deep-fried flounder. First the cook stuffs a dried hot pepper into a radish. Then the chile-filled radish is grated and becomes a nippy garnish.

Then there's Htipiti, a cheese spread popular in Salonika, Greece. Two chopped hot chiles are beaten into half a pound of feta cheese until the cheese grows fiery enough to ignite the eater's tastebuds. Or a Serbian recipe called Farmer's Caviar, made from eggplant and hot yellow chiles (those same chiles that we know in the Southwest as Güeros). Or Sarsuela, a fish stew from Catalonia, which blends hot chile powder, mild chile powder, and red Bell peppers, according to the tastebuds of the diners and the chef. Or the Brazilian recipe for Môlho de Pimenta e Limão. This salsa combines four Tabasco peppers with half a cup of chopped onion and half a cup of fresh lemon juice to create fluid fire.

Closer to home, the O'odham Indians of Arizona and Sonora, Mexico, make a relish of bacon, green chiles, tomatoes, and onion. They cook the dethorned buds of the cholla cactus with chiles. They mash green chiles into a pulp, shape them into pancakes, and dry them outdoors in the sun.

Recipes that use chiles in unexpected ways intrigue me most. Check the hundreds of cookbooks of nouvelle cuisine, ethnic dining, and hot and spicy foods that came out in the eighties and early nineties, and you'll find recipes for chile strudel, chile milkshakes, chile mayonnaise, Jalapeño hollandaise, chile pesto, chile syrup, and candied Chipotles. In just one of these cookbooks, Georgeanne Brennan and Charlotte Glenn's *Peppers Hot and Chile*, come recipes for chile cream sauce, squab seasoned with Serranos, chile-glazed prunes, dandelion greens seasoned with roasted Poblanos, mushrooms livened with chiles, chile figs, and even a recipe that combines the tastes of chiles and corn fungus.

It's difficult to find a food product that doesn't also come doctored with chiles. You can eat fiery cookies. Chew sizzling almonds. Crunch mouth-blasting peanut brittle. Spoon up hot ice cream. Lick Habanero lollipops.

A Eugene, Oregon, company fills chocolates with salsa. In West Rockport, Maine, the Spruce Mountain Blueberry Company makes a spicy spread, which I like to slather on pancakes, from wild blueberries and hot peppers. If you visit the Mt. Horeb Mustard Museum in Mt. Horeb, Wisconsin, you'll see one hundred chile-enhanced mustards among the 1,500 mustard types.

Even such old-fashioned staples as peanut butter and jelly now come doctored with capsaicinoids. Next thing you know, Kellogg's will sell tingling Cornflakes.

Sometimes chile enthusiasts grumble about this explosive inventiveness. But even the most outrageous chile dishes and concoctions develop logically from the try-anything philosophy that comes from eating chiles in the first place. And a lot of these inventions aren't really so different from what the Aztecs ate. Besides that, there's some evidence that chiles don't just wake up your tastebuds. They keep them awake, so that you can enjoy more the other flavors which accompany or follow chiles.

My own favorite chile dish is a Southwest traditional, the cholesterol-loaded chile relleno (stuffed chile). I've eaten chiles rellenos all across the Southwest, from Texas to California, but I've never found one tastier than at Chope's, a café in the village of La Mesa in southern New Mexico.

In the scant three and a half hours during which proprietors Cecilia Yañez and her sisters admit lunch and dinner guests daily, they serve three hundred to four hundred chiles rellenos. The tiny two-room restaurant, which features formica-topped tables and linoleum-tiled floors, began as their

At chili cookoffs around the country, judges taste the first helping of each contestant's chili, and spectators get the rest. Here, Dick Chenevey of Phoenix, Arizona, ladles out samples. Like other chili enthusiasts, he and his wife Cece tinker endlessly with their recipes. "Sometimes I even cook in my dreams," he says.

Above: With genetic engineering, sweet Bell peppers come in every color of the rainbow but blue. Shepherd's Garden Seeds of Torrington, Connecticut, sells a packet called "The Rainbow Pepper Collection" with seeds for orange-, red-, violet-, and ivory-colored bells. If left on the plant to ripen, the Bell peppers shown here, which go by the name Islander, will change from purple to red.

Right: In 1986 chile scholar Janet Long-Solís wrote of the name Cayenne, "The use of this term is currently being abandoned because it is considered confusing and imprecise." The problem is that the spice industry invented the name in order to indicate any very hot, intensely red pepper, no matter what its shape or size. The name survives, however, and has been adopted by those who categorize chiles into pod types. Distinguishing characteristics of the pod type: very hot, and very red.

family home. On some weekends sixty years ago, their boot-legging grandmother would hang out a lantern to let people know she also had enchiladas for sale.

One day recently I followed Cecilia into the kitchen and watched as Mexican-born Cristina Garcilazo, a petite, sixtyish widow and mother of ten, got ready for the evening whirlwind of diners. She first learned to cook rellenos from Cecilia's mother, Lupe Benavídez, who still lives in the house and presides over Chope's. "Nobody can do it like I can," Garcilazo announced proudly in Spanish, as she showed us the green chiles she'd spent all afternoon preparing. In the top of each chile, which had already been roasted and peeled before it reached Garcilazo, she had snipped a hole, then inserted a long piece of cheddar cheese.

As I watched, she whipped the whites of five dozen eggs until they were fluffy, and, at the very last minute, added the yolks. "That's one of the secrets," she observed. "Some people add the yolks too soon, or don't add them at all."

Next, Garcilazo dipped the chiles in flour. After that, she pulled them lightly through the egg mixture to coat them with fluff. Then she fried them in very hot lard until they turned golden brown.

Perhaps it was the lard. Perhaps it was the experience Garcilazo had gained from preparing ninety thousand chiles rellenos a year. But when I sat down to eat, I knew she was right. Those golden, virtually greaseless chiles rellenos were the best chile dish anyone could ever hope to dine on. And it may just have been my imagination, but it really did seem

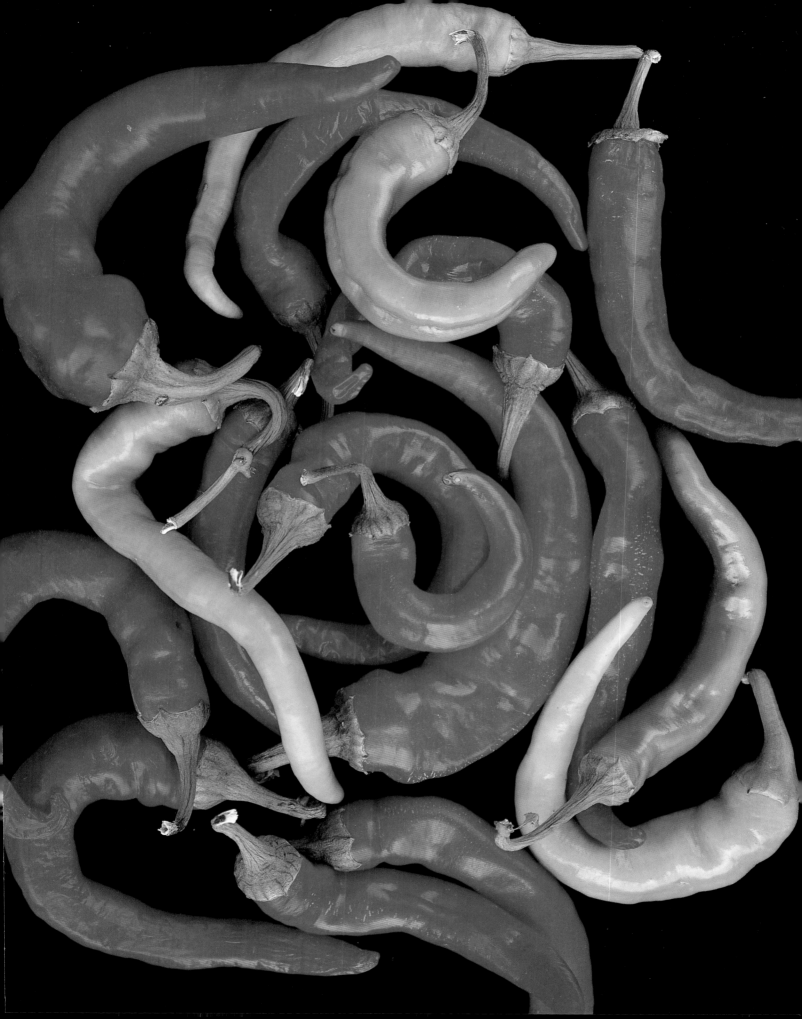

SIZZLING SALSA

2 small or one large tomato
9 green Serrano or Serranito peppers
1 small or 1/2 large red Bell pepper
1/2 medium onion
6 stalks cilantro
2 cloves garlic
1/2 cup water
2 Tablespoons red wine vinegar
2 teaspoons canola or corn oil
1/2 teaspoon salt

Cut the tomatoes in fourths. Wearing rubber gloves, remove and discard the stems of the Serrano peppers, then cut them in halves. Cut the red Bell and the onion in fourths. Remove the leaves from the cilantro stalks and discard the stalks. Place the tomatoes, Serranos, Bell pepper, onion, cilantro leaves, and garlic in a blender. Add water and vinegar and chop at medium speed just until the mixture is reduced to small chunks. Add oil to a stainless steel skillet and pour the salsa mixture in. Add salt. Bring to a low boil. Continue to cook at a low boil for four or five minutes, stirring frequently. Cool and store in a covered jar in the refrigerator. Can be used as a dip with chips or as a sauce on chiles rellenos or other dishes.

For a milder salsa, reduce the number of peppers. For a thicker salsa, reduce the amount of water.

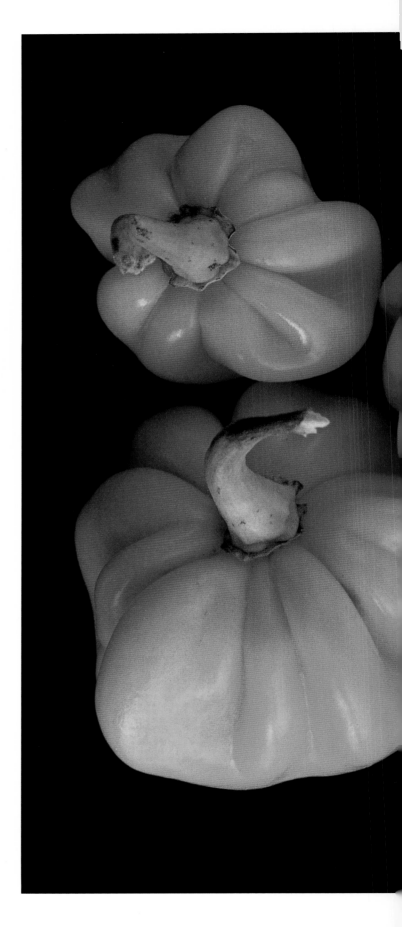

Experts look for an indented ridge near the base of the stem to distinguish the *Capsicum chinense* peppers shown at right from their *Capsicum annuum* lookalikes, Squash peppers. The other sure test is to taste them. Squash peppers are nonpungent. Their *chinense* twins, which in the Caribbean typically go by no more exact name than Hot Peppers, create the culinary version of a nuclear meltdown in the mouth.

Above: Across the United States and elsewhere, some lucky schoolchildren come home to snacks like this: Blistering chile peanut butter and fiery chile jelly coat slices of spicy chile bread.

Right: New Mexico leads the United States in production of hot peppers. Most of the state's chiles go by the general name New Mexico chiles, although cooks often stick to the old-fashioned names Green Chile and Red Chile. Elsewhere, people call these same chiles Anaheims or Californios. Here three curling New Mexico chiles illustrate the visual poetry that draws the eye to chile peppers. The chile pepper craze has been compared to bird watching—with the added advantage that you can eat the pepper when you've finished admiring it.

to me that I could taste the rest of the meal—rice, sopaipillas, cheese, chips, and a soft drink—more intensely than I ever had before.

A raven hopped up on the windowsill and watched me eat the last bite.

I wondered if he was jealous.

Animals, after all, have strong opinions about the culinary values of peppers, too. Birds of all sorts, including magpies and wild turkeys, gobble chiles. Ants, however, avoid powdered chile, perhaps because it diverts them from their work. Bedbugs flee the smoke of burning chiles. (Of course, so do would-be sleepers.) Coyotes so detest chiles that nineteenth-century shepherds scared coyotes off by sprinkling their sheep with chile powder. Sharks are said to find peppers so unpleasant that some sea-going Indians of Central America protect themselves from sharks by trailing ristras in

the water. (Too bad the old man in the *Old Man and the Sea* didn't know that.)

Amal Naj, author of *Peppers, a Story of Hot Pursuits*, swears that once in Bolivia he saw a bee coat itself carefully with chile powder. But the most remarkable account of chile-related animal behavior I've ever seen comes from historian Hubert Howe Bancroft, who wrote in the 1880s, "I am seriously informed by a Spanish gentleman who resided for many years in Mexico, and was an officer in Maximilian's army, that while the wolves would feed upon the dead bodies of the French that lay all night upon the battlefield, they never touched the bodies of the Mexicans, because the flesh of the latter was completely impregnated with chile."

It's all just more fodder for the eons-old gustatory ballad of the chile pepper.

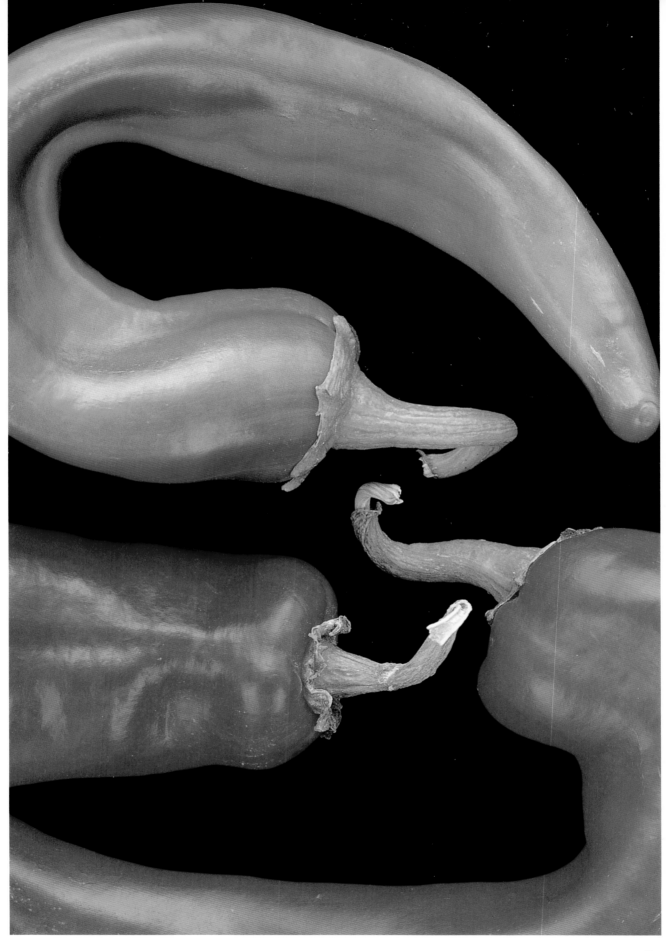

Above: From September through December workers at Biad Chile Company in southern New Mexico process up to 4,500 pounds of fresh chiles an hour. Here, New Mexico chiles wait to pass through the drying chambers. On the other side, they'll be crisp and dry—and, without any additives whatsoever, they'll taste like spicy candy.

Left: How to douse the fire of chile peppers? Folk remedies range from bananas to beer, and from potatoes to pears. Miguel Araujo, shown here eating—and reacting to—Habaneros, reports that in the Yucatan, where he grew up, people eat warmed tortillas or sprinkle salt on the back of their hands and lick it off. Scientists recommend milk because a protein in milk cuts the effects of capsaicinoids much as a detergent cuts grease. Most chile writers point out that since capsaicinoids don't dissolve in water, as they do in alcohol, water doesn't work. But in Mexico, ancestral home of peppers, an old folk saying claims water is the best antidote. Someday scientists may find out why.

Each February manufacturers of fiery foods from the United States, Canada, and the Caribbean gather in Albuquerque, New Mexico, for the National Fiery Foods Show. At one recent show visitors sampled salsas from Alberta, Maryland, Washington state, Connecticut, the Virgin Islands, and a dozen other locales. They sipped chile beer from Arizona and sampled jerk sauce from Trinidad. The author reports that her personal favorites were the Popcorn de Macho from Cavanna Foods of San Antonio, Texas, and the Premium Chunky Hot Salsa from Piada Foods of Coleman, Texas.

While gathering data for her book *The Beautiful and the Dangerous*, anthropologist Barbara Tedlock visited Zuni Pueblo in western New Mexico, home to the Zuni Indians. Among the dishes she ate were raw Jalapeños and roasted New Mexico green chiles. One day some mourning doves flew past, and Tedlock asked her host if the Zunis ate the birds.

"Sure," he said, "when I was growing up we had a lot of dove chili stew, but it's not eaten so much these days."

These Poblano peppers would be just right for those who like their chili stew mild.

PIQUANCY: TWO PEPPERS

THE WOODCHUCK'S CLAM CHOWDER

1 10-ounce can of whole baby clams
2 fresh Güero (Yellow Hot) peppers
2¼ cups water
1/2 medium onion
1 Tablespoon olive or canola oil
2 potatoes, diced
1 teaspoon dried parsley
2 3/4 cups milk
salt and black pepper to taste

Drain and rinse the clams, discarding juice. Wearing rubber gloves, wash the peppers and remove the stems. Pour the water into a two-quart saucepan, add the peppers, and simmer for five minutes. Sauté the onion in the oil. Add clams, potatoes, parsley, and sautéed onions to the water and cook for about fifteen minutes, or until a fork goes through the pieces of potato easily. Add milk and salt and pepper to taste. Cook on low heat for five more minutes. Cool and let sit a day in the refrigerator.

Just before serving, remove and discard the peppers. Makes four bowls (approximately six cups) of chowder. Serve with Red Hot Cornbread (page 117). For hotter chowder, add an extra pepper.

These nonpungent peppers, a variety of *Capsicum annuum,* take the name Mushroom chiles from their shape. Yellow Mushroom peppers look so much like blastingly hot Scotch Bonnet peppers from the Caribbean that it takes an expert to distinguish them just from their appearance. But break the two peppers open, and the difference is clear. Scotch Bonnets, a variety of *Capsicum chinense,* have a fragrance that Mushrooms lack, and Bonnets rate a ten on the Official Chile Heat Scale, compared to Mushrooms' zero. The similarity suggests opportunities for practical jokes: Help yourself to a yellow Mushroom, and offer a Scotch Bonnet to a friend. Then run for your life.

ح   ح   ح

"I heard a Spaniard from Mexico say that it was very good for the sight, so he used to eat two roast peppers as a sort of dessert after every meal."

—GARCILASO DE LA VEGA, 1609

In the 1700s, Jesuit missionaries in the Americas wrote about the customs and lifestyles of the peoples they encountered. Some Jesuits reported that ristras like these were an essential part of everyday life. Ristras provided chiles for stews all winter. They doubled as an all-purpose medicine cabinet. And people used them as money to buy other foods and products.

LIVE HOT OR DIE:
A Cure for What Ails You

 OKAY. YOU'VE EATEN YOUR WAY FROM COAST TO COAST OR continent to continent at chili cookoffs and restaurants large and small. You've added chiles to all the recipes on stained three-by-five cards in your old wooden recipe box, from Annette's Apple Brown Betty to Zella's Never-Fail Pie Crust. You've done nasty little animal experiments in which you forcefed chiles to neighborhood creatures from cockroaches to cats. What's left?

Everything.

For instance: medical and therapeutic uses for chile. In every culture that has ever adopted chiles as a food, the shiny pods have worked their way quickly up from the spice rack to the medicine shelf.

Consider my own modest, but real, experiences using the Chile de Arbol as a home remedy.

This Mexican chile rates 15,000–30,000 Scoville Units or seven on the Official Chile Heat Scale, two steps up from the Jalapeño, a step up from the Serrano. I first encountered it in a beachside hotel in the Mexican state of Guerrero. It was late September, but already at 7:00 A.M., the air had that hot, humid feeling which, as the day passes, makes a person tired and groggy. While I and other travelers ate our breakfasts in the open-air dining room, where indoors and outdoors merged, a young hotel employee named Josefina stood working at a *molcajete*, a traditional grinding stone.

I walked over to take a look. She was crushing chiles, tomatoes, and onions together to make the day's salsas. The chiles were slender, and a deep red, and they ranged from about an inch and a half to five inches long. The shortest resembled Texas Chile Piquíns, a cultivated variety of the wild Chiltepín. The longest resembled small Cayennes.

"What kind of chiles are those?" I asked.

Above: Medical studies confirm what Spanish colonists and their descendants have known for centuries: Capsaicinoids can reduce the pain of arthritis. The medical cure involves a cream made from a dilution of capsaicinoids. In the folk cure, the patient wears a chile-vinegar compress. Both treatments can produce a mild to strong burning sensation on the skin, and neither is recommended without first consulting a physician. Shown here: a sampling of medicinal and culinary pepper products from around the world.

Left: Across the Southwest each autumn, people who work seasonally as chile roasters set up in grocery store parking lots. When a shopper comes out with a fifty-pound gunnysack of chiles, the roaster tosses them into the wire-mesh drum and turns on the propane jets. As the drum rotates and the chiles tumble, the skins char and loosen for easy removal later. Here, flames fly skyward as chiles roast in Eloy, Arizona.

"Chiles de Arbol. Sometimes we call them Rat's Tail chile because that's what they look like."

"How hot are they?"

Josefina smiled. "They are terribly hot, Señora. We like them here in Mexico. They help keep us awake." She shrugged. "But I think they are probably too *picoso* for North Americans."

Later that day, in the marketplace, when I began to feel logy, I remembered Josefina and bit into a Chile de Arbol. After a moment's delay, my entire mouth began to burn so intensely that I dropped the rest of the chile and fled to find a drink. I was awake, all right, but I was too distracted to notice.

It was a long time before I tried another Chile de Arbol. When I did, the sensation was still so strong that it focused my total attention on the pain in my mouth.

Eventually I adjusted to that spreading burn, and began using it to treat my natural afternoon energy sag. Sometimes when I start feeling headachy or have trouble concentrating about 3:00 P.M., I pull out a few dried Chiles de Arbol and set them beside my word processor. At the very first bite, the initial sting of the chile focuses all my attention, and after the intensity passes, my lips, tongue, and palate tingle pleasantly for several minutes. After that, I find I can concentrate better and work more quickly.

This same remedy has been reported in Bolivia, where people sometimes keep themselves awake by putting crushed chiles between their gum and cheek.

Columbus initiated the first Western propagandizing about chiles when he wrote to Ferdinand and Isabella in 1493 that "the meat they eat with very hot spices"—probably some sort of chili stew—helped New World natives endure severely cold weather in the mountains.

That claim was tame. A folk cure from the Caribbean advises men who are losing their hair to rub chile-impregnated oil into their scalps. A folk tradition from the U.S. Southeast alleges that you can cure poor circulation in your extremities—and therefore, warm cold feet—by sprinkling chile powder in your socks. Texas cattle drivers used to swear that eating chiles could counteract rabies. Householders in some parts of India believe that if you hang a ristra of green chiles outside the entry to a house, you can avoid ailments caused by the evil eye. (Red chiles don't work.) Traditional Hungarian folk medicine advises sprinkling chile powder on wounds to prevent infections. From Africa come reports that eating red chiles will, first, cure your hemorrhoids, and then keep you eternally young. (Green chiles don't work.)

Do you suffer from yellow fever? Malaria? Kidney failure? Apoplexy? Cancer? Heart disease? Spring fever? The common cold? Have you been rejected in love? Has a witch put a hex on you? Do you have the seven-year itch? Are your fingers swollen and twisted with arthritis? Do you suffer from one intense headache after another, day after day? Would you like to lose weight? Or perhaps you're reading this in the middle of childbirth and find that, although you've been in labor for hours, the baby still hasn't come?

The cure, my friends, is always the same. Peppers. Peppers. Peppers. Eat them. Breathe them. Rub them on your skin. And like some Biblical sufferer, you'll be able to take up your bed and walk and be whole again.

In fact, the medical and therapeutic claims for chiles from culture to culture and century to century are so extensive and diverse that it would be easy to conclude that capsaicinoids affect the same part of the mind that novelists aim at: the part that causes the "willing suspension of disbelief."

Or, as H. Allen Smith might have put it: Eating chiles will make your brain so soft, you'll believe anything.

However, before you vow never to eat another chile, lest your own brain, too, should turn to mush, consider this: Every year medical science either validates more of these folk claims or makes new claims that no one had even thought of before.

While more and more North Americans and Europeans were transforming their tentative love affairs with chiles into a life-time relationship in the 1980s and early 1990s, medical researchers were doing more and more tests of the medical effects of capsaicinoids. In 1990 and 1991 alone, researchers reported on over one hundred clinical studies on human subjects; another five hundred studies tested laboratory animals. As a 1990 article in the Journal of the American Medical Association put it, "This active agent in Tabasco sauce is becoming a common condiment in many basic science laboratories."

Scientific findings may be drier than folk claims, but they are equally remarkable.

Medical researchers at the Institute for Clinical Medicine in Italy, at Case Western Reserve University in Cleveland, Ohio, and at other institutions have used topical creams that contain capsaicinoids to treat arthritis. By rubbing capsaicinoid creams on arthritic knees or hands, patients with osteoarthritis were able to reduce pain by one-third. For patients with rheumatoid arthritis, the pain declined by more than one-half.

Above: These ornamental *annuums* change from purple to yellow to orange to red as they ripen. Paul Bosland, who developed them for decorative use as potted plants or in formal gardens, calls them NuMex Twilight. Like other ornamental peppers, they're edible, but lack the complex combination of tastes and textures that add to the culinary appeal of most peppers. Fiery hot, ornamental *annuums* may end up seasoning a stew.

Left: Traditionally, most chile ristras have been made of dried red New Mexico chiles. These days, though, ristra makers try all types of peppers. The ristra at right uses a small hot chile. The ristra on the left is made from ristra chiles developed by Paul Bosland. Yellow chiles are NuMex Sunglo, red are NuMex Sunflare, and orange are NuMex Sunburst.

Meanwhile, investigators at the pain clinic at Toronto General Hospital in Canada searched for a way to treat prolonged cases of shingles, a viral condition related to chickenpox that affects more than 300,000 North Americans each year. In about fifteen percent of cases, the disease includes a chronic phase of severe ongoing pain called postherpetic neuralgia. Just the touch of a bedsheet can hurt so much that the patient cannot sleep. When the Toronto researchers applied a capsaicinoid-based cream to their patients' shingles-sensitized skin, 78 percent of the subjects experienced some decrease in pain, and 56 percent noticed a substantial decline.

Others studies show that capsaicinoid creams can reduce or eliminate trigeminal neuralgia, a severe pain near the corner of the mouth or the nose. The creams can lessen or stop intense limb pain caused by diabetic neuropathy. People who experience severe itches with medical names like pruritus, notalgia parasthetica, and lichen simplex chronicus improve with these treatments, too. The ointments appear to work partly because capsaicinoids interfere with the nerves' ability to transmit pain messages to the brain.

Capsaicinoid nasal sprays work, too. Researchers at the University of Florence in Italy used capsaicinoid sprays to treat the intense pain of cluster headaches, which can attack day after day for weeks or months. The pain concentrates on one side of the head, typically around an eye. In the Italian study, a nasal spray containing capsaicinoids was squirted into one nostril of twenty-nine cluster headache sufferers. Thirteen subjects received the spray in the nostril opposite the side of the head that felt the pain, and they experienced

Children from Hatch, New Mexico, created these whimsical chile dolls. Hatch, home of hot Hatch green chile, calls itself the Chile Capital of the world. That's more poetry than fact. Towns in India, Mexico, Korea, China, Thailand, and elsewhere could all claim that title with equal justification.

A young woman in Ballet Folklorico costume rides a float in the shape of a red New Mexico chile during October's annual Whole Enchilada Festival in Las Cruces, New Mexico. Following the parade, a local restaurateur cooks the world's largest enchilada, ten feet in diameter, in the middle of the street in front of city hall. As anyone who has ever eaten an enchilada might guess, the linguistic and culinary root of the word *enchilada* is *chile*.

PIQUANCY: FIVE PEPPERS

HORS D'OEUVRES FROM HELL (FOR HABANERO ADDICTS ONLY)

one batch of pastry dough (page 80)
2 12-ounce jars of whole Habanero peppers
1 8-ounce package of regular or low-fat cream cheese
1/2 cup low-fat or nonfat sour cream
1 teaspoon dried parsley flakes
2 ounces unsalted, unoiled cashew nuts, chopped fine
1/8 teaspoon salt
1/8 teaspoon coarse-grind black pepper
approximately 1/8 cup water
approximately 1/8 cup milk

Make pastry dough, following directions on page 80, and refrigerate for one hour.

Wear rubber gloves and work outdoors or in a well-ventilated kitchen. Pour off the vinegar in which the Habaneros are packed and save it to use in seasoning salads. Rinse the peppers well several times in water, remove and discard the stems and seeds, and set the peppers aside on paper towels to dry.

Mix the cream cheese and sour cream together thoroughly. Add parsley, chopped cashews, salt, and black pepper and stir until well blended. Using an espresso spoon or your gloved fingers, stuff the Habaneros with this mixture.

Roll the pastry dough out thin, and use a cup or lid to cut it into circles approximately three and one-half inches in diameter. Place one stuffed Habanero in each circle. With your finger, apply a light coating of water to the edge of the dough, fold over, and seal. Prick an air hole in the top of each tart.

Place the tarts on a greased cookie sheet and bake at 450 degrees until crust is golden brown (approximately fifteen minutes). About five minutes before they are finished, brush the top of each tart lightly with milk; discard any remaining milk. Remove tarts from the oven and allow to cool for up to two hours before serving. Makes approximately fifty hors d'oeuvres.

CAUTION: Habaneros are the hottest peppers on earth, so save these hors d'oeuvres for a gathering of Habanero addicts. First-time Habanero eaters should nibble one cautious bite at a time and stop by the end of the first tart.

no improvement in their headaches. But the remaining sixteen subjects received the treatment in the nostril on the same side of the head as the headache. In eleven subjects, the headaches stopped completely, and in two more, the number of headaches was cut in half.

Other researchers have found that capsaicinoid nasal sprays can reduce or cure severe chronic allergic and nonallergic conditions that make the subjects' noses run constantly and cause them to sneeze frequently. The physiological mechanisms behind such cures are not clearly understood.

Medical studies also show that eating chiles can improve your health. Research in New Mexico and Thailand, two hotbeds of chile consumption, suggests that eating chiles lowers the risk of heart disease. That may be because capsaicinoids can lower cholesterol and triglycerides, without affecting "good" cholesterol (HDL). Capsaicinoids also help the body metabolize fat. And they appear to work as a natural anticoagulant to help prevent blood clots.

Other medical research suggests that eating chiles can reduce the risk of lung diseases. A diet rich in chiles may also prevent or slow the development of some cancers, apparently because of the antioxidant effects of capsaicinoids.

Most medical research lumps all capsaicinoids together, but some studies test the effects of one particular capsaicinoid. In one case, for instance, researchers found that dihydrocapsaicin in particular helped guinea pigs' bodies offset the effects of a cholesterol-rich diet.

Hungarian medical researcher Albert Szent-Györgyi was studying chile peppers in the early 1930s when he discovered and isolated vitamin C, which earned him a Nobel Prize. Chiles, it turns out, contain even more vitamin C per unit weight than oranges do. That may explain why early Spanish sailors instinctively chose pickled peppers to take along on extended trips: The chiles prevented scurvy, a disease that is caused by lack of vitamin C and was once common among sailors.

Chiles are also high in vitamin A, which, studies suggest, can improve night vision. That justifies the Spaniard

Ristras count among the most popular items at chile stores and gift shops across the United States. But Habanero products now outsell even ristras. When customers began asking for Habanero peppers in the late 1980s, virtually none were available. So Stonewall, Texas, farmer Jeff Campbell decided to grow them himself. Now he harvests up to 60,000 pounds of Habaneros each season and produces a line of Habanero products including hard Habanero candy.

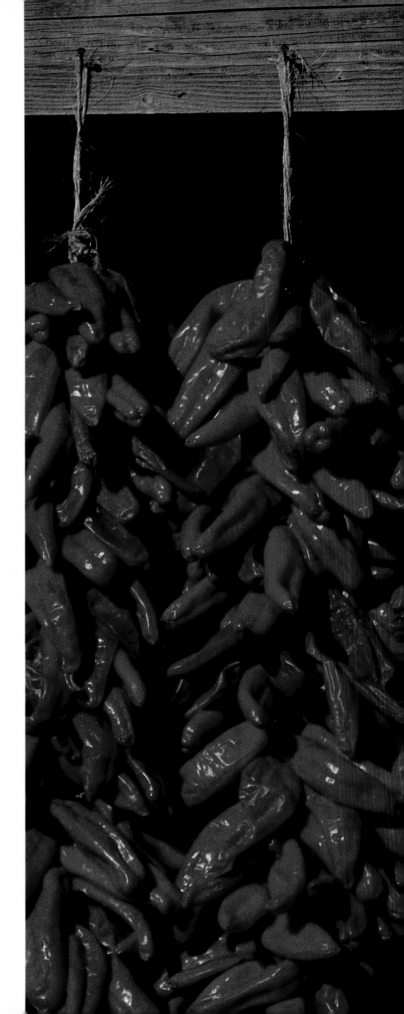

HOT CHERRY PIE

pastry dough:
1 2/3 cups flour
1/8 teaspoon salt
1 4-ounce stick of butter or margarine
1/3 cup milk
filling:
2 canned green Tabasco peppers, packed in vinegar
2 Tablespoons cognac
2 16-ounce packages of frozen pitted tart pie cherries
1 1/3 cups sugar
6–8 Tablespoons quick cooking (Minute) tapioca
1 Tablespoon vanilla
glaze:
approximately 1/8 cup milk

Two days before you plan to make the pie, place two Tabasco peppers in a narrow jar and add two tablespoons of cognac. (The peppers should be nearly covered with cognac.) Cover and set aside at room temperature.

For crust: Mix flour and salt. Work the margarine or butter into the flour mixture. Add milk and mix just until the dough comes together and can be formed easily into a ball. Refrigerate for at least an hour before rolling out.

To make the filling, empty cherries into the top part of a double boiler, add sugar and six tablespoons of tapioca, and stir well. Heat in a double boiler over low heat until cherries are warm and juicy. Remove from heat. Dif-

ferent brands of frozen cherries have different moisture content; if cherries seem quite juicy, or if you like a firmer pie, add the remaining two tablespoons of tapioca. Remove the peppers from the cognac and discard them. Add the cognac and vanilla to the heated cherries, stirring very well to insure even heat distribution in the pie.

Divide the dough into two portions. Roll out the bottom crust, lay it in a nine-inch pie pan, prick it well with a fork, and bake for ten minutes at 400 degrees. Remove from oven and add the heated cherry filling. Roll out the top crust. Moisten the rim of the bottom crust lightly with water and apply the top crust, pressing the two together with your fingers or the underside of a fork. Trim away overhanging dough and discard. Cut two or more air holes near the center of the top crust. Bake the pie at 400 degrees for ten minutes, then turn oven down to 350 and cook for another hour or until filling starts bubbling through the air hole. About fifteen minutes before pie is done, brush a light coating of milk over the top crust. Repeat procedure five minutes later; discard any leftover milk.

For a milder pie, use just one pepper; for a hotter pie, add two teaspoons of the vinegar the peppers are packed in before you add the vanilla. May be served with whipped cream or vanilla ice cream.

whom half-Incan, half-Spanish writer Garcilaso de la Vega described in 1609: "I heard a Spaniard from Mexico say that it was very good for the sight, so he used to eat two roast peppers as a sort of dessert after every meal."

Sounds as if, at last, we've found a box to put chiles into. Right?

Wrong.

As dazzling as all the medical findings are, an undertone of contradiction accompanies them. In high doses, capsaicinoids can function as a neurotoxin. Other research suggests that, although eating chiles reduces overall cancer risks, too many can actually increase the chances of colon cancer. It also turns out that chiles may be mildly addictive, apparently because they start a chain reaction that stimulates the brain to release endorphins, the body's natural painkillers. This may be why, as Chileheads know, the more chiles you eat, the more you want to eat them. However, medically

speaking, eating chiles in excess is out, unless, say, you're trying to win the Laredo, Texas, Jalapeño-chomping contest some February.

Medical experts urge people not to use capsaicinoid ointments or nasal sprays as home remedies, either. That's partly because, in spite of their medical benefits, capsaicinoids can burn and sting.

Consider what happens when you roast your own green chiles.

I roasted chiles for the first time shortly after I moved to Santa Fe in 1980. My neighbor Rose, whose family has been eating chiles in New Mexico for four centuries, told me exactly what to do: Roast the chiles in a well-ventilated place, preferably outdoors, and above all, put on rubber gloves before peeling them.

I listened politely, and then did it my way. I put the chiles in a pan and set them under the broiler of the oven in

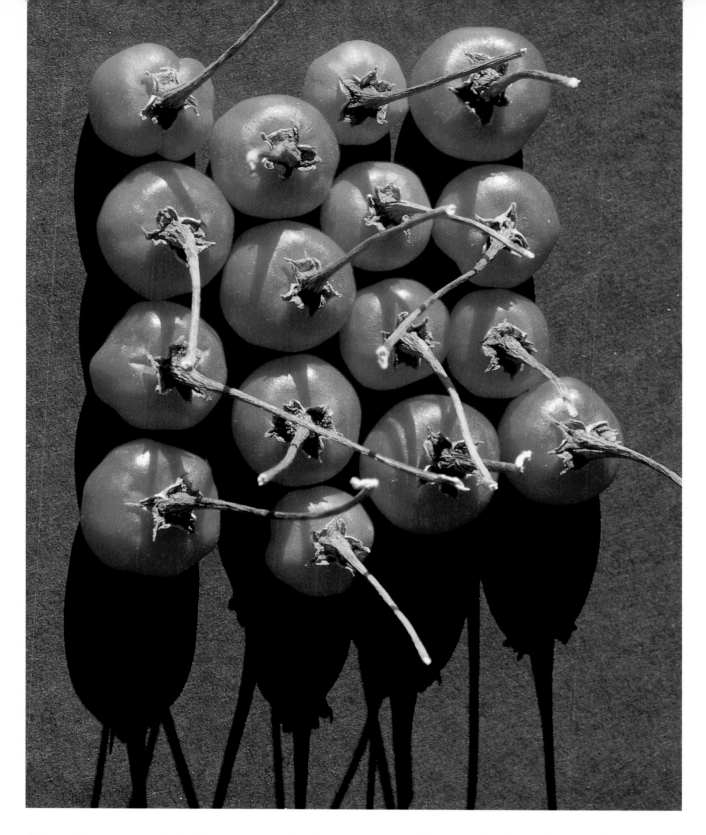

Folk medicine has prescribed chiles as a panacea for hundreds and probably thousands of years. But nobody recommends eating chiles excessively. In 1992 Israeli physicians reported a case in which a man, 23, ate twenty-five hot peppers in twelve minutes. Four hours later, he entered the hospital with excruciating abdominal pain. During surgery, physicians discovered a five-millimeter hole in the intestinal wall. Their conclusion: Capsaicinoids in the peppers had contributed to the rupture. The hot *Capsicum baccatum* peppers shown here come from Brazil, home to hundreds of varieties of domesticated and wild peppers.

Today we have the luxury of using chiles for decorations like these chile wreaths. Spanish colonists had to be more practical—and more inventive. When colonists moved into the U.S. Southwest, bedbugs tortured them. The historical record is vague, but it is likely that the scratching colonists tried many remedies before they found one that worked: They burned the veins and seeds of chiles as a fumigant. The bedbugs fled. Once the colonists stopped coughing and sneezing, they slept in peace.

my poorly ventilated kitchen. Then I sat on a nearby stool to watch and wait. About the time the chiles started to sizzle and pop, I started coughing and sneezing. My nose began running so hard, I looked as if I were about the third day into a worst-case cold.

I was beginning to realize that Rose was right. But since I didn't have any rubber gloves, I went ahead and pulled the skin off the roasted chiles with my fingers. Within about a minute, a stinging sensation spread across my hands. Twenty-four hours later, my skin was still burning intermittently.

Another time my son broke open an Habanero with bare fingers and absentmindedly touched his face and neck. Within minutes his hands, face, nose, and neck began burning severely. Two hours later he was still checking the mirror to reassure himself that his face was still there.

In November 1992, a *Newsweek* article described a form of torture reportedly used in a Mexico City prison to force prisoners to confess to crimes. It's called *tehuacanazo*, and it involves spraying a mixture of chile powder and seltzer water up the subject's nose. Not so different from the techniques of medical researchers, you might argue, except that in medical studies, subjects are usually anesthetized first. Still, as monstrous as *tehuacanazo* sounds, it's simply a variation on ancient traditions. Pre-conquest Indians of Mexico punished their children by forcing them to breathe the smoke of roasting chiles. And they punished sex crimes by rubbing crushed chiles on the offending parts of the anatomy.

Chiles' functions as a medicine and a tool for molding behavior don't end the list of possible uses. Farmers sometimes add byproducts of mild chiles to chickenfeed to make yolks a brighter yellow. Doing the same to a canary's food can make the bird's feathers turn yellower. Colors extracted from chiles brighten lipsticks, sausages, and salad dressings. Read the fine print on a can of commercial antiattacker spray, and you may discover it's one of the brands that use capsaicinoids as the active ingredient. You'd be spraying—and immobilizing—an attacker with chiles.

For centuries people have used chiles in place of cash.

In pre-Columbian Mexico, Indians paid their taxes in chiles. After the Spanish took over from the Aztecs, the conquerors continued to accept chiles as taxes. In northern New Mexico in the late 1700s, with one ristra of chiles you could buy a deerskin, a pair of shoes, a pound of chocolate, three dozen eggs, a yard of linen, or a nannygoat. As late as the early 1900s, you could still use a string of ristras in southern Colorado or northern New Mexico to purchase such staples as beans (one ristra bought eight pounds) or wheat (one ristra bought twenty pounds).

Chiles serve a literary function, too. Writers as diverse as Amy Tan, Martin Cruz Smith, Marc Talbert, and Zora Neale Hurston have seasoned their fiction with chiles. In the fiction-devouring decades before and after World War I, writers like Amanda Mathews Chase and Lucia E. Smith sometimes used chiles, or chili stew, as a major ingredient in their short stories. But the most famous literary use of chiles comes from master storyteller O. Henry, who wrote a fictional piece about the chili stew of San Antonio, Texas.

In this story, "The Enchanted Kiss," a chili lover named Tansey meets a man named Ramón Torres, who claims to know of a secret food that has kept him alive, and youthful, for four hundred years.

Asks Tansey, "And this health-food you spoke of?"

Replies Torres: "Eet is the chili-con-carne made not from the beef or the chicken but from the flesh of the señorita—young and tender. That ees the secret. Everee month you must eat it, having care to do so before the moon is full, and you will not die any times."

You'll have to read the story to find out what Tansey, and Torres, ate next.

It's illegal to practice medicine without a license. So unlike O. Henry, I won't offer any prescriptions. But if I did, I'd say next time anything ails you, take two Chiles de Arbol and go out and have a good time. And oh, yes, that advice will cost you two ristras of chile, payable at the time of your visit to my office, unless prior arrangements have been made.

Red chiles, please. Green ones won't do.

Dietitian Nancy Gerlach, co-author of *The Whole Chile Pepper Book* and food editor of *Chile Pepper* magazine, travels the world in search of exotic peppers and pepper dishes. But she reports that her favorite chiles remain Chipotles (smoked Jalapeños) and New Mexico chiles like the ones shown here. "New Mexico chiles add a lot of flavor to a dish without adding a lot of heat," she says, "and Chipotles with their smokiness are wonderful in barbecue sauces."

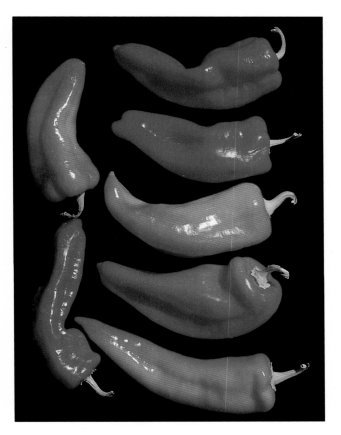

Chile aficionados have developed many remedies for the burning sensations that may occur when capsaicinoids touch the skin. Chile writer Beth Dooley reports that when she asked immigrants from Southeast Asia about their remedies, a Laotian woman in Minnesota told her, "Rub salt in your belly button. It's an old family secret." Other remedies include rubbing the affected area with vegetable shortening, alcohol, lemon juice, or a diluted bleach solution. With repeated exposure, the skin adapts to capsaicinoids, and chile lovers like Susan Zamora can peel roasted chiles safely without gloves.

These sweet peppers, a variety of *Capsicum annuum* called Cubanelle or Cubanella, are popular in stirfry dishes. They rate zero on the Official Chile Heat Scale. Chile writer Dave DeWitt, who popularized that scale, decided to rate peppers and recipes on a simpler continuum that reflects the impressionistic nature of piquancy ratings. Categories in the new method: mild, medium, hot, and extremely hot.

Left: The taxonomists who named *Capsicum pubescens* were feeling playful: They called it *pubescens* because the leaves are hairy. *Pubescens* peppers grow at high elevations in Central and South America, and moved northward only in the past century. Mexicans call the *pubescens* chile shown here Manzana because it resembles an apple. In Central America the same chile goes by the name Caballo chile because, when you eat it, it feels as if a horse has kicked you.

§ § §

"Just between you and me, I'm a little suspicious of any state where they eat the decor."

—JOHN KELSO, 1992

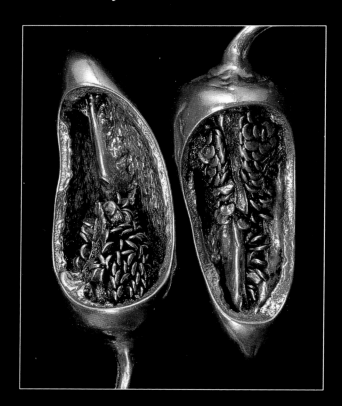

When artist T. Kern Hicks started casting bronze chiles in the 1980s, he had to overcome a series of technical problems with the molds, which he makes from fresh chiles. "If I didn't apply the ceramic shell fast enough, the fresh chile would dehydrate," he recounts. So he learned to wax the pepper first, then apply the ceramic. He uses fresh Güeros and Jalapeños as models for his lifelike cutaway chiles.

CHILE MANIA:
From Fishing Lures to Fine Art

 A SHALLOW EARTHENWARE BOWL ABOUT SIX INCHES ACROSS
sat on a bookshelf in an office at the University of California at Los Angeles. Around the
outside of the bowl, the artist had swept his paintbrush in a few graceful lines to create images
of chiles. His style suggested training in both Minimalism and Expressionism.

Chris Donnan, director of UCLA's Fowler Museum of Cultural History, lifted the bowl
carefully and set it on the coffee table in front of us. The clay-slip paint looked so fresh that
Donnan could have said, "The artist brought this bowl in last week." Instead, he said, "This
is a Nazca bowl from Peru. It probably dates from about 300 or 400 A.D. The ancient Peruvians left no written record, but their ceramics help us reconstruct their cultural history." The
bowl is one more proof of the importance early Peruvians placed on peppers.

Seeing that bowl made me want to explore the connections between peppers and what
sociologists call contemporary popular culture—the customs, beliefs, values, attitudes, and
artifacts of everyday life.

I soon found plenty for future anthropologists to uncover in our rubble. Button covers in
the shape of chiles. Blouses, trousers, aprons, and hats made from chile-pattern prints. T-
shirts covered with chile designs. Underwear decorated with chiles. Striptease dancers' pasties
from which miniature ristras dangle. (These artifacts will surely earn the notation "function
and use unknown.") Table lamps shaped like chiles. Wind socks that resemble chiles. Door
handles that look like chiles. Tote bags decorated with cloth chiles. Chile keyrings. Chile pot
holders. Chile bird houses. Ornamental tiles depicting chiles. Chile-decorated stationary.
Swizzle sticks, fishing lures, watches, dog toys—all shaped like chiles.

In some households, even Christmas has become a chile-heated holiday. You can hang
Christmas wreaths made in Arizona from intertwined chiles. You can package your presents
in chile-paper wrapping made in California or Texas. Or brighten your Christmas tree with

Above: Approximately sixteen centuries ago a Nazca artist in Peru painted chiles on this bowl from the collection of the Fowler Museum of Cultural History at the University of California in Los Angeles. Pre-Columbian artifacts throughout Latin America illustrate the importance of chile peppers in everyday life.

Right: In this 1988 vase, Navajo artist R.C. Gorman combines two of the most evocative symbols of the Southwest: an Indian woman and chile peppers.

ornaments and lights shaped like chiles, made by companies from as far away as Taiwan. Or create that evocative Southwest Christmas glow by placing sand and a candle in a chile-decorated bag from Minnesota. Or cut Christmas cookies with chile cookie cutters made in Texas. Or eat Christmas dinner on chile placemats handwoven in India. For a few years in the late 1980s, while a student in New Mexico was sewing his way through law school, you could even allow the children to wait by the fireplace for San Capsico (or Santa Claus, whoever arrived first), in cozy sleeping bags that resembled chile pods.

If you lined up all the items that look like chiles or use real chiles decoratively, they would probably stretch from the unknown South American birthplace of chiles to any household on earth where Chileheads live. A couple of thousand years from now, when future anthropologists look at the art and artifacts we leave behind, they'll probably conclude that in the late twentieth century, the chile pepper

was, if not actually a god, then perhaps an intermediary between humans and gods. Or they may decide, as I have, that nonfood chile products are simply props in the ongoing Theater of the Absurd which is life.

Part of this craze, which has been called Chile Pepper Fever, Chile Madness, and a few other names, includes the blossoming of retail shops selling chile-related products.

SuAnne Armstrong, who grew up in New Orleans, opened the Chile Shop in Santa Fe, New Mexico, in 1985. It was, she believes, the first store of its kind in the United States, combining a full selection of chile edibles with a full range of chile kitsch. Over the years, Armstrong has added nonchile items with a general Southwest theme to her stock, but the store continues to emphasize chile foods and nonfoods.

"Some of this can get real hokey," she told me one day. I tried not to smile. "But it can also be fun and in good taste. Look at this." She held up a bright red dinner bell in the shape of a chile; it had a green top and red clapper. "Some-

Art critics argue among themselves about where to place the works of Navajo artist R.C. Gorman, who has grown famous with his flowing depictions of Navajo women. Meanwhile, Gorman's works hang in galleries and homes around the world. This limited edition lithograph, entitled "Chimayo Chiles," is one of several Gorman lithographs of chiles.

Loretta Valdez of Velarde, New Mexico, shown here with one of her chile wreaths, considers the local land race of chiles too tasty—and too rare—to use in anything but cooking. So she and her employees work with less exotic varieties of New Mexico chiles to create her popular chile decor.

BAKED CHILES RELLENOS

11 egg whites
2 egg yolks
12 fresh New Mexico (Anaheim) green chiles
approximately 3/4 pound mozzarella, asadero, or
    other cheese
3 Tablespoons flour
1/4 teaspoon salt
1/8 teaspoon pepper
1 ounce grated Parmesan cheese

Place egg whites in one mixing bowl and yolks in another and set aside to warm at room temperature.

Roast the chiles under the broiler, turning occasionally, until the skin browns evenly (a stainless steel pan works well). Allow them to cool, then remove the skins and stems. (If you are not used to cooking with peppers, leave the kitchen window open for good ventilation and use rubber gloves when handling the chiles.) Whole canned chiles may be substituted for fresh; drain them well and pat dry with paper towels.

Cut the mozzarella or asadero cheese into slices approximately half an inch wide, half an inch thick, and five inches long (about half an inch shorter than the chiles). Cut a one-inch hole near the top of each chile and insert a slice of the cheese. If the chiles have developed tears or holes, simply drape the chile around the cheese.

Beat the egg whites to a soft peak stage. Sprinkle in the flour and continue to beat until well blended. Add the egg yolks, salt, and pepper and beat a few more seconds, just until well blended. Sprinkle the Parmesan cheese on the egg mixture and fold in gently for approximately eight strokes, or just until barely blended.

Dip each stuffed chile carefully in the egg mixture so that the chile is heavily coated. Place on a greased glass or stainless steel baking pan, spacing the chiles three inches apart. Discard any extra egg mixture, or spoon it on top of the chiles.

Bake at 425 degrees for fifteen minutes or until the coating turns golden brown. Serve at once. To spice up this dish, serve topped with warmed Sizzling Salsa (page 60). To cool it down, serve topped with sour cream.

thing like this might sound silly, but it's actually quite well done. And people really seem to connect with this kind of stuff."

Since 1985, other stores packed with chile salsas, chile powders, chile foods, and chile kitsch have opened in places like Texas, Missouri, Kansas, Arizona, Massachusetts, Louisiana, and New York. In addition, dozens of gift shops, kitchen shops, and specialty stores across the country have added chile theme products to their lines. In Santa Fe, which is, admittedly, a stronghold of chile products, lore, and kitsch, you can buy chile-related items ranging from ceramic recipe-card holders to coffee mugs in more than a dozen stores. The Coyote Café General Store has even started a salsa-of-the-month club, in which members receive one salsa or hot sauce each month, with recipes to match.

In San Antonio, Texas, five members of the Rivera family, together with their employees, run Rivera's Chile Shop, which has one of the most diverse selections of chile merchandise in the country. Among the most popular items are ristras made of ceramic chiles and piñatas shaped like chiles. "One woman even came in one day to buy a piñata to wear as a costume," says Irma Rivera. But, apart from chile t-shirts, the most popular clothing item of all, at $7.95, is a woman's halter top, in a chile print, made from men's underwear.

"People from places like Oregon and North Carolina come to us and say they'd like to open a franchise of our store," says Rivera. "But we're just not up to doing that."

In Boston, Lisa Lamme, owner of Le Saucier, sells sauces and condiments of all sorts, with an emphasis on hot chile sauces from thirty-eight countries. She also sells chile t-shirts, pickled Chile Piquíns, chile powders, and so on. When she opened in 1988, Le Saucier was such a novelty for the East Coast that radio stations, television crews, and newspaper and magazine writers swept into the store, creating a flood of more than three hundred media reports on Lamme and Le Saucier. Now the people who show up with videocameras more often hope to steal trade secrets. Lamme generally shoos them out, but she gladly shares some of what she's learned. "The hotter, the better, is the key to selling," she says. "And I'm not sure what this means, but there are a lot of doctors and lawyers who really like it hot."

In her advertising Lamme dares people to come in and try the hottest sauce.

Hearing about the dare, people ask, "What do I get?"

"A hot mouth," she tells them. "And satisfaction." (That may be what the early Peruvians were thinking about when they identified chiles and satisfaction, Uchu and Sauca, as brothers.)

People often ask Lamme, "What do you have for my mother-in-law?"

Lamme's standard reply: "Do you like your mother-in-law or don't you?"

Lamme has worked her way up the Official Chile Heat Scale to the point that she now sprinkles powdered Scotch Bonnet peppers on her clam chowder. But she displays a prominent sign in her store that says, EAT AT YOUR OWN RISK. And she entertains herself by watching people who try to act tough when they sample her hottest salsas.

"I have people who come in and taste things that I know are too hot to bear. There's nothing wrong with saying, 'This is too hot for me.' Instead, they'll say casually, 'That's not so hot.' But I can always tell." She watches for a blushlike spot that appears behind the exaggerator's ears within about sixteen seconds of downing a mouthful that's too hot.

In Kansas City, R.J. Samuels is a chile people watcher, too. After seeing the way people took to chiles and salsas in his five Mexican restaurants, he and two partners opened chile-filled stores called Lotta Hotta in Overland Park, Kansas; Kansas City, Missouri; and St. Louis, Missouri. They sell chile t-shirts, chile baseball hats, chile stationary, and so on. But above all, they sell salsas and other chile-laced foods, all of which they invite customers to sample.

"I'm past being surprised about who likes to eat hot," Samuels says. "A little kid will come in here, maybe seven, eight years old, and he'll want to sample something I think is way too hot." Samuels tells the young customer to ask his parents first.

"So the kid comes back trailing his parents, and they say, 'Oh, yes, let him try anything he wants. You won't believe how hot he can stand it.' And they're right. Sometimes it's the kids who can eat the hottest stuff of all."

But Samuels still likes to be cautious. The day after he opened his first store, a customer came in and said, "Give me the hottest stuff you've got."

Samuels did: a tiny sample of blazing Habanero sauce.

These small peppers, an ornamental *Capsicum annuum*, change hues several times as they mature. Colors in these and other chiles result from the interaction of three pairs of genes, plus a chlorophyll retainer gene. There is no correlation between color and pungency, but peppers which have reached their final color (usually red) may taste slightly less biting than at earlier stages because their natural sugars have developed completely.

"Give me some more," the man demanded.

Samuels did.

All of a sudden the man turned red. He started coughing and choking and hyperventilating. "It took him forever to settle down," Samuels reminisces, "I really thought that guy was going to die on us. I'll never do that again." Now he encourages people to start with Jalapeños and work their way up.

In New York City, David Jenkins, owner of Hot Stuff Spicy Food Store, imports thirty-gallon drums full of Scotch Bonnet pepper sauce from Trinidad and packages it under his own label.

In the two years since he opened, Jenkins has been surprised to find who his customers are: "They're seventy percent males. Mostly white. But about the only thing they have in common is that they seem to prefer products with the word *hell* in the name."

Mark Miller, founder of the Coyote Café and the Red Sage Restaurant and author of *The Great Chile Book,* may have an explanation for that. His theory is that, for men at least, eating hot is a way of proving their masculinity. "You could say that eating chiles is macho."

That doesn't explain women like me, who eat peppers hotter than we can stand just for the sake of doing it. Or maybe it does. Maybe, for us, this is all connected on some deep level to that Jungian need to find and unite the male and female sides of ourselves.

Just as they did in pre-Columbian Peru, chile peppers have caught the attention of serious artists and artisans.

In New Orleans, jewelry artist Mignon Faget, a sixth-generation Louisianan who has designed jewelry for more than two decades, creates sterling silver bracelets from which forty-eight silver Tabasco peppers dangle. Each bracelet sells for $1,250. Faget also designs pepper cufflinks, tie tacks, tuxedo studs, earrings, and pendants in both silver and gold.

"In my jewelry I like to concentrate on things from the environment I grew up in," she explains. "In Louisiana we're very big on peppers and spices. I grew up eating this wonderful hot stuff. When I put peppers on a bracelet, they look like the strings of hot peppers you can buy in the market." When *Chile Pepper* magazine ran a two-sentence item about her work, Faget began receiving calls from all across the United States and Canada.

Two Seattle glass artists, Joey Kirkpatrick and Flora Mace, started a trend when they began shaping molten glass into chiles that sell for up to $8,000 each. Seeing their work, another Seattle glass artist, Paul Cunningham, developed a line of eight-inch-high handblown glass goblets with red chiles for stems; the goblets sell for $200 each.

Navajo artist R.C. Gorman creates lithographs in which pensive Navajo women make chile ristras, hold chiles, or sit dreaming next to baskets of chiles. The limited-edition prints sell for around $1,800, almost as fast as galleries can hang them. Other New Mexico artists sculpt chile pods from pine wood or pour molten bronze into molds that leave weighty chile peppers behind.

A little less seriously, and a little more downscale, El Paso, Texas, artist Gregory Cook has used chile sauce to paint political cartoons. At last report they weren't for sale.

My own favorite chile art is an untitled acrylic painting by Paul Souza. Souza, who taught for many years at the Art Center College of Design in Pasadena, California, grew up in Hawaii, where chiles brightened local gardens. "I don't know what kind of peppers they were," he says today, "but I know they were hot. Something like Tabasco peppers. When my mother caught me swearing in Pidgin English—or any other language—she'd wash my mouth out with one of those nasty little peppers."

In Souza's pepper painting, three red New Mexico chiles hang suspended, with their shadows, in a sea of white space. It would be easy to wax philosophical and say the painting symbolizes the completeness of chile peppers and their effects on their surroundings. But Souza is more poetic, and more practical. "Chiles are like cats," he says. "We know that we need them, but they'd never let us know that they need us."

The most widespread visual use of chiles in the United States is also one of the oldest: chiles in ristras and wreaths, which the owners of chile shops across the country report as one of their best-selling items.

Because of the bountiful supplies of chiles in New Mexico and the dryness of the air, most chile ristras and wreaths in the United States are made in New Mexico.

One day I drove north from Santa Fe to the village of Velarde to visit Loretta Valdez, who is probably the best known wreath maker in North America. Her chile wreaths range from under a foot in diameter to more than twelve feet across. She lives in an area where Spanish colonists began growing chiles four centuries ago. The descendants of those chiles have developed into a distinct land race, called

New Orleans jewelry artist Mignon Faget created these sterling silver peppers to honor the historic role of peppers in the folk culture of Louisiana.

Above: Holiday lights in the shape of red and green chile peppers have become so popular at Christmas that they are now manufactured overseas for import to the United States. When they've finished opening their presents, chile aficionados can sit around the tree and debate whether the chile lights, which come in several styles, look more like Serranos or Jalapeños.

Left: The RC Company of Rush City, Minnesota, developed these chile-decorated *luminaria* bags to light the night on Christmas Eve. Orders come from around the United States and Canada, with heaviest sales in the Southwest. "We wanted something that would say Southwest to people," RC general manager Jim Ertz explains, "and chiles were one of the four symbolic images chosen." The others were coyotes, skulls, and cacti.

Velarde, that varies from standard New Mexico chiles by having square shoulders, thinner walls, and, say its advocates, a better taste.

I found Valdez and several helpers working in a house that had been converted into a combination studio, workshop, and showroom. On the walls hung simple wreaths made of chiles, corn, and grasses, and ornate wreaths that included peacock feathers, Hopi kachina dolls, and the ribboned masks worn by Matachines dancers.

Many of Valdez's chile creations bore a printed statement that identified them as Ramona Love Letters. "When I was growing up, we lived in California for a while," the native New Mexican explained, "and I was intrigued by the hanging corn, which some people called Ramona Love Letters." She wanted to know what that meant, so she searched until she found Helen Hunt Jackson's novel *Ramona.*

"Ramona's lover would leave her a gourd or an ear of corn to let her know where they would meet. I told myself, if Ramona had lived in New Mexico, her lover would have left her a chile as a message to meet him in the chile field." So when Valdez started making wreaths from chiles, she called them Ramona Love Letters.

"My wreaths are for all seasons," said the petite mother of five and grandmother of seven, who first began combining chiles, corns, and grasses into wreaths back in 1968. "Of course, the local chiles are too delicious, and too scarce, to use for wreaths. I feel it's sinful." Sometimes she uses Cayennes. "I tried using red Jalapeños, but they cracked when they dried. And after the first year, Chiles de Arbol fade too much." Finally she settled on Sandías, a lively New Mexico chile that rates four on the Official Chile Heat Scale, as her number-one wreath chile.

She and the villagers she employs make ristras from Sandía chiles, too. "It's a medium-hot chile," she explained. "That way, if they want to pick a chile off the ristra and use it in their food, they have a perfect chile, not too hot, not too mild, to throw into the stew."

Chile lore and chile news fuel several periodicals. In Texas, Jo Ann Horton and Judy Wimberly produce the *Goat Gap Gazette*, a tabloid-sized newspaper with a circulation of five thousand, eleven times a year. The Chili Appreciation Society International publishes another Texas newspaper, *Terlingua Trails.* In California, the International Chili Society publishes a quarterly sixty-page newspaper and an annual magazine. All four publications concentrate on chili stew and cookoffs.

The New Mexico-based *Chile Pepper* magazine has a much broader focus: anything that has to do with chile peppers in any form around the world. Magazine subscribers live primarily in North America.

If the circulation of *Chile Pepper* is any indication, then chile mania has just begun. The magazine started in 1987 with 225 subscribers. By January 1990, circulation had blossomed to ten thousand. By January 1993, it had climbed to eighty thousand.

One day I visited the editor, Dave DeWitt, at the magazine's headquarters in Albuquerque, where chile products from all over the world line desktops and bookshelves. He sat in an office surrounded by back issues of the magazine, which have become so scarce that collectors pay six dollars for a photocopy.

"How much of this is just a fad, and how much of it reflects an actual change in our cultural values?" I asked.

"I'm always amused at people who say chiles are a fad," he answered, fiddling with a rubber stamp that leaves the imprint of a chile ristra. "If they are, then they've been a fad for about ten thousand years."

"But what about all the chile kitsch and chile art?"

He shrugged. "Nobody knows. My own sense is that the retail stores, for instance, could be part of a fad. But it's probably just beginning. There are thirteen chile stores across the U.S. now, and I expect to see that figure reach a hundred before the trend passes. It may not pass, though, at least any time soon. You'd be astonished at the mail I get. I think a lot of people have been secret Chileheads for years, and they're only now coming out of the closet. Certainly it's obvious that chiles symbolize something to people. Chiles remind people that they like to feel daring."

That was what prompted Georgians Mary Sue Onyon and her husband Richard to name his Atlanta-based computer software firm the Chili Pepper Software Company. "In the software business people are conservative," says Mary Sue. "But we didn't want anything stuffy. We wanted something fresh, something that conveyed energy, and that's when we thought of peppers." Now people tease the couple, whose last name sounds like Onion, about the vegetable connection.

That's just the sort of lighthearted news that makes the pages of *Chile Pepper* magazine. While a layer of seriousness lurks behind some articles, humour and whimsy predominate. The "Hot Flash" news items include such tidbits as the lethal dose of Louisiana hot sauce—one quart, according to a toxicology magazine report. Cartoons carry captions like this: "Tiburon, California's main street was evacuated when

PIQUANCY: FOUR PEPPERS

FROZEN FIRE
(HOT POPSICLES)

3 fresh Güeros (Yellow Hots)
5 cups water
11.5-ounce can of frozen cranberry juice concentrate

Wash the Güeros and cut off the stems, leaving the rest of the pepper intact. Add the Güeros to the water and bring them to a low boil. Simmer, covered, for twenty-five minutes, then remove from heat and allow to cool. Remove and discard the Güeros. If any seeds remain in the water, strain them out. Combine the water and the frozen juice concentrate in a pitcher. Mix well. Pour into popsicle molds and freeze for after-school treats. Or pour into ice-cube trays and use as ice for soft drinks. The juice may also be served unfrozen, as a lively cold drink.

Above: Jan and Dirk Schneider, owners of the Chili Pepper Emporium in Albuquerque, New Mexico, stock their two shops with about 50 percent food items and 50 percent nonfood items—all related to chile peppers. "The thing I like best," says Jan, "is that chile is fun. People are in a good mood when they come in here." Shown here: the Schneiders' store in Albuquerque's Old Town.

Left: Chile expert Dave DeWitt would like to bring order to the chaos of chile nomenclature. He would particularly like to systematize and standardize pod types. "I like to think we could do for chiles what has been done with the names of dogs," he says. "The pod types would equal the standard breeds of dogs. For instance, a Jalapeño would be like a collie. The varieties of Jalapeños, such as TAM Mild and Mitla, would be like the variations within a breed, such as, say, Shetland collies." One major problem: So many peppers are mutts.

Right: For centuries artists have practiced technique by painting still lifes of fruits and vegetables. If Paul Gauguin or other nineteenth-century European artists who favored still lifes had painted the peppers shown here, more diners in Europe might have discovered the culinary pleasures of hot peppers.

Above: Chile shop owners report that ceramic kitchenwares painted with chile motifs or shaped like chiles are among their best-selling nonfood items. Ceramicist Ann Marie Eldridge created this top-selling line of soup tureens and attached soup bowls.

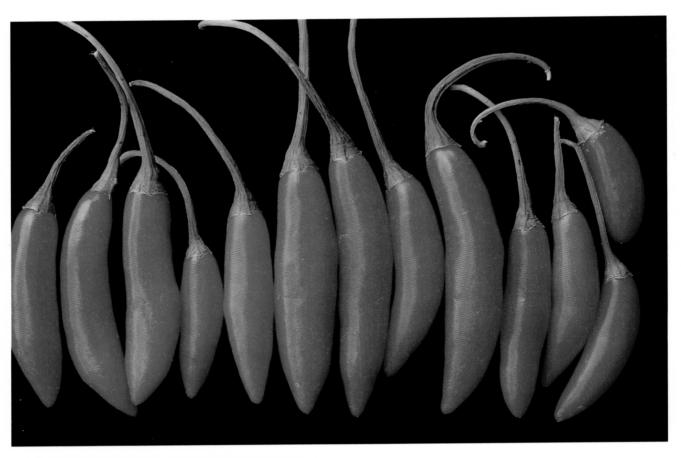

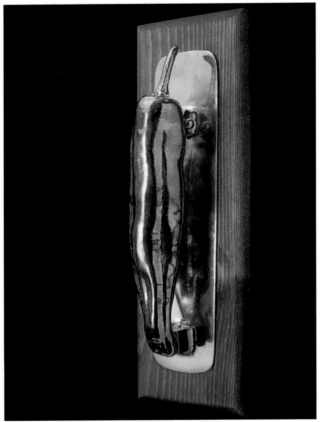

Above: As peppers spread through the popular culture, they become part of popular literature, too. In the best-selling novel *Red Square,* Martin Cruz Smith's Russian investigator Arkady Renko visits a bar where the new elite of the former Soviet Union can pass their time sipping pepper vodka. The ornamental *annuums* shown here are probably hot enough to become a plausible murder weapon in a contemporary thriller.

Left: Chile shops and gift stores sell chile-inspired knick-knacks, souvenirs, and home furnishings. In designing the door knocker shown here, T. Kern Hicks hunted for the perfect New Mexico chile, then made a rubber mold that he could use again and again. Sociologists and students of popular culture wonder whether the public's attraction to such objects is only a passing fad or part of a long-term shift in interests and values.

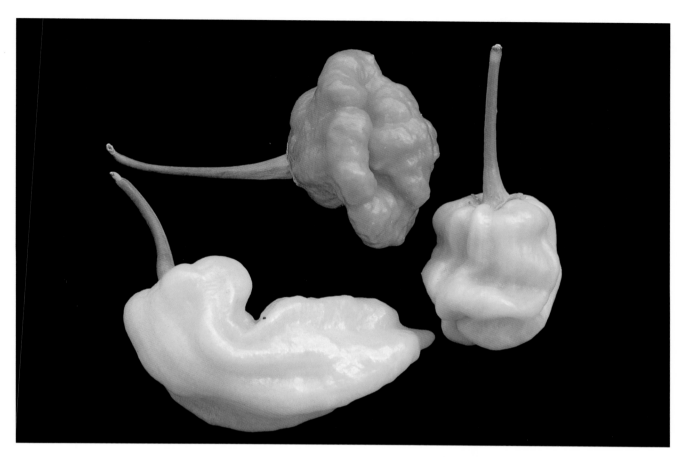

Above: Habaneros and Scotch Bonnets are the two most famous varieties of *Capsicum chinense*. But in St. Augustine, Florida, only one variety counts: the small Datil pepper. Christopher Way, CEO and Chief Pepper Picker at the Datil Pepper World Headquarters in St. Augustine, has devised a special method of growing the Datils on elevated platforms that make picking faster and easier. Harvest begins in May and continues all summer long. The *chinense* peppers shown here come from the Caribbean.

Right: Houston, Texas, writer Jennifer Farley has called North Americans' blossoming love of hot peppers "politically correct thrill seeking" and "the dining room equivalent of bungee jumping." Shown here: Peppers hot enough to make you want to jump off the restaurant roof.

officials thought the aroma of roasting chiles was a toxic leak." And its articles carry titles like "Do the Jerk." (That headed a food piece on pepper-propelled Jamaican jerk food by food editor Nancy Gerlach.) Read half a dozen issues, and you'll begin to suspect that while it's an attachment to chiles that draws people to *Chile Pepper* magazine to begin with, it's the lightheartedness and exuberance of the writing that keeps them coming back.

But perhaps the best example of the ways in which chile and people combine to form humor comes from the pages of the *Austin American-Statesman* of Austin, Texas. One day in August 1992, columnist John Kelso fired the ultimate bullet at New Mexico from the Texas side of the Great Chile War. Never mind that he has never set foot in New Mexico, or that he acknowledges, "I don't know a thing about peppers."

Discussing ristras, and their dual role as stew enhancers and room decoration, he wrote, "Just between you and me, I'm a little suspicious of any state where they eat the decor."

Yes, on some levels the chile pepper's involvement in popular culture borders on silliness. But maybe the same thing was true in ancient Peru.

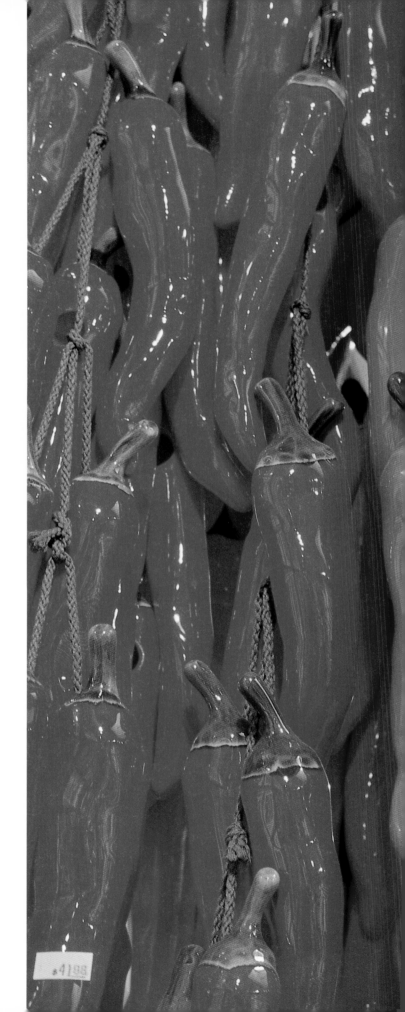

Like ristras of real chiles, ceramic chile ristras come in oranges, yellows, reds, and browns. Outdoors, they double as wind chimes. Indoors, they maintain their shape and color long after natural ristras fade.

᷎   ᷎   ᷎

"The seedes hereof must be sowen in a bed of hot horse dung."
—JOHN GERARD, 1597

Most chiles change color as they ripen. But few change as spectacularly as this variety of *Capsicum chinense*, which is seen here shifting from green through orange to red. Photographer Eduardo Fuss says the color change took place so rapidly that when he checked the pepper the day after this photograph was taken, the fruit had lost all its green.

DOWN ON THE FARM:
The Importance of Being Chile

 THE GREAT CHILE WAR, OF COURSE, IS MORE HUMOR THAN WAR. Apart from those few cannonading chiles, it consists mostly of newspaper columns and light-hearted proclamations and resolutions full of *whereas*'s and *be it resolved*'s.

However, chile breeder Ben Villalon, of Texas A&M University's Agricultural Experiment Station in Weslaco, Texas, takes the Great Chile War seriously. And he doesn't like it. "I tried to tell those guys up in Austin and other places that it's ridiculous to compete with the farmers of New Mexico. We complement each other. We don't need to compete."

Season after season Villalon crossbreeds peppers for specific traits. He works to improve their resistance to plant diseases and to create tastes, colors, and shapes that please processors and eaters.

I'm no fan of genetic tinkering, and my first instinct is to question the wisdom of that sort of work. But the fact is, left on their own, chiles crossbreed furiously. If you planted New Mexico 6–4s, Jalapeños, Güeritos, Serranos, and Bell peppers all together in one field, then collected and planted their seeds, they would mix and match and change their colors, shapes, heat, and sizes with every generation. Within a few seasons, all by themselves, they could create dozens of new chile types.

Villalon, Bosland, and breeders who work for private industry systematize and channel this natural genetic exuberance. In fact, that may be one reason people domesticated Capsicums so early. It wasn't that they loved chiles so much; they were just trying to bring them under some kind of control.

When Villalon created the TAM Mild Jalapeño-l, which contains only one-third the heat of a normal Jalapeño, it allowed salsa companies to standardize the heat levels of their products. They could start with a base of TAM Mild Jalapeños, and add carefully regulated amounts of hotter Jalapeños to create hotter sauces. "It changed the way the salsa companies

Above: As the Río Grande flows through New Mexico and Texas, it passes fields of Güeros, Bells, New Mexico chiles, Jalapeños, Cherry peppers, and other Capsicums. In southern New Mexico, Las Cruces, shown here with the sunrise glinting on the Río Grande, lies at the heart of the number-one chile producing region in the United States. To honor Capsicums, the Chile Institute, based at New Mexico State University in Las Cruces, proposes to build a Chile Pepper Museum. Hundreds of varieties of peppers will grow in the demonstration garden. The museum shop will sell chile pepper books, seeds, and gifts. Exhibits will illustrate the history of peppers and their uses in science, industry, and medicine.

Left: As the chile harvest advances, farmers around the world watch their fields for signs of chile wilt, which causes millions of dollars in crop damage each year. Meanwhile, as the rain forests of Latin America disappear, so do the species of wild chiles that grow in them. In Guatemala, chile researchers fear that the wild species *Capsicum lanceolatum* has become extinct. Because the pepper evolved in a wet environment, it probably developed resistance to chile wilt. If breeders could obtain some seed from *C. lanceolatum,* they might be able to produce domesticated hybrid chiles that would resist this destructive fungus.

operated," Villalon says with satisfaction. "They started using a lot fewer tomatoes, and a lot more peppers."

Besides the TAM Mild Jalapeño-1, for which he is famous, Villalon has created a new kind of Güerito, the TAM Rio Grande Gold Sweet. It looks like the hot Santa Fe Grande, but, like a Bell pepper, it lacks the gene that produces capsaicinoids. He developed a medium-sized disease-resistant Bell, the TAM Bell-2, which farmers in Venezuela and Hawaii grow. He has also invented two new hot Jalapeños, the TAM Veracruz Jalapeño, which produces three times more fruits than ordinary Jalapeños, and the TAM Jaloro, a yellow Jalapeño. The TAM Veracruz, he believes, will prove resistant to most major chile viruses, and early tests show that the TAM Jaloro contains 60 percent more vitamin C than regular green Jalapeños. "These will probably replace all the other hot Jalapeños," he predicts, as proudly as if he were a parent talking about twin sons who had been nominated together to become Supreme Court justices. And even though Villalon professes disgust at the Great Chile War, he just happens to be working on a new long New Mexico-type chile, which he tentatively calls the Tex-Mex 6. This pepper, he hopes, will be so superior to the New Mexico 6–4 and similar New Mexico chiles, that farmers in New Mexico will switch.

"I'm thinking only of the best interests of the farmers and producers and consumers," he insists.

Even if Villalon should turn out to be a secret soldier in the chile war, he's right. New Mexico and Texas complement each other in terms of chile crops. To begin with, Texas farmers plant mostly Jalapeños and Bells; New Mexicans grow mostly New Mexico types (often called Anaheims elsewhere) and Cayennes. The seasons are different, too. South Texas is so warm that peppers grow there year-round. Farmers plant in January. Hot nights in March and April make the peppers mature quickly. Field hands begin picking ripe chiles in May. By June the harvest ends, and by July 1 farmers are planting their second crop.

Meanwhile, in southern New Mexico, the first chiles begin ripening in late July, when fewer Texas chiles are available. The second harvest in southern Texas doesn't begin until the harvest in New Mexico slows down in November.

Chiles can grow in almost any part of the United States or southern Canada, and, contrary to John Gerard's 1597 advice, they don't need to start life in a bed of hot horse dung. They thrive in areas with cool nights and warm days that don't become unbearably hot. For reasons that are still not understood, virtually any stress—poor soil, high night temperatures, too much rain, too little rain—will cause a chile plant to increase capsaicinoid production.

Take the same strain of seeds and plant them in the same garden, year after year, and some years the harvest will be noticeably hotter than others. Or take carefully certified, identical seeds and plant them in two different locations, and they'll probably produce chiles of somewhat different piquancy. That's one reason why chile lovers often prefer chiles grown in a particular place. In the mid-1800s, for instance, John Russell Bartlett reported that in the Santa Cruz Valley of southern Arizona red chile grew "in perfection, and is said to be preferred on account of its superior piquancy to any raised in Sonora."

Partly because of climate and growing conditions, and partly for cultural and historical reasons, the five major pepper producing states in the United States were all once part of the Spanish colonial empire. The United States Department of Agriculture does not keep records on pepper crops, and state records are scanty, but it's generally agreed that New Mexico leads, followed by California, Florida, Texas, and Arizona. In 1991 New Mexico farmers grew 373,000 tons of chiles on 30,000 acres. Two-thirds of those acres lie in the southern counties of Luna and Doña Ana.

Emma Jean Apodaca-Cervantes is one of the leading farmers in Doña Ana County, where 1,100 farms fill 100,000 acres of low-lying land in the Mesilla Valley on either side of the Río Grande as it heads south towards Mexico.

One day I drove out to see Apodaca-Cervantes. It was 105 degrees on a late morning in September. Shimmery currents of heat wavered up past adobe row houses, past signs that read U-Pick Chiles, past a store that does a dual business in grave markers and chile ristras. In 1598, Spanish colonists rode their horses along this route as they headed north to establish the first European settlement in what is now the U.S. Southwest. Some of Apodaca-Cervantes's ancestors rode with them.

I joined Apodaca-Cervantes, who is slim, attractive, and fiftyish, at the twenty-room, two-story adobe hacienda her farmer father built fifty years ago. From there we drove out to her chile fields. As we bounced along the one-lane farm roads that lace the Mesilla Valley together, she talked about her life as a chile farmer.

"This chile war with Texas keeps us on our toes," she said with a laugh that suggested she was joking. "But with or without that, the most important thing we have to consider is the needs and tastes of our buyers." She sells long New Mexico green chiles to restaurants for chiles rellenos and

Above: Except for McIlhenny's Tabasco sauce, most Louisiana-style hot sauces use Cayenne peppers. Many of Louisiana's Cayennes grow in New Mexico. Here a harvester in one of Emma Jean Apodaca-Cervantes's fields empties a bucket of Cayennes into a holding bin in the early morning light.

Left: Emma Jean Apodaca-Cervantes, one of the leading chile farmers in New Mexico's Mesilla Valley, still makes her own chiles rellenos. To reduce cholesterol, she fries them in vegetable oil instead of lard, and she uses only one egg yolk for every three egg whites.

Right: When they dry, these bright red chiles retain their smooth skin and shape, and the seeds inside them shake with a rattling sound that gives them their name: Cascabel. At 20,000 Scoville units—seven on the Official Chile Heat Scale—this pepper seems medium hot to some eaters, scorchingly hot to others.

For all the romance of peppers, harvesting them requires long hours of exhausting labor. Here a farm worker in California walks through a field of Güeros on his way to the holding bin.

other dishes. She sells green Jalapeños to processors in Louisiana, California, and Texas. She packages and sells vine-dried New Mexico red chiles directly to the public. But more than anything else, she sells a salted mash made from ripe red Cayennes to processors in Louisiana, who use it to make Louisiana-style hot sauces.

"Being a chile farmer is a year-round job," she said. "In December and January, when our crews finish picking the last sundried red chiles, we're out hustling as hard as we can to line up next season's contracts." She seldom plants a chile that isn't already spoken for. By the time she tucks the first chile seed into the earth in her greenhouses in February, she knows exactly how much land she'll need on planting day, St. Joseph's Day, March 19.

"This year I planted five hundred acres of my own land in chiles and subcontracted with farmers for another 1,100 acres," she said. "I could have planted more of my own land, but chile is one of those crops that need to rotate. You get your best yield when you wait three years before planting a field with chiles again."

Weevils, worms, viruses, and fungi all feed as enthusias-tically on chiles as people do. Rotating fields helps reduce these pests.

"It also helps us fight what I like to call the AIDS of chiles," she continued. "Chile wilt." A fungus that lives in the soil and thrives on moisture causes this bane. When the summer rains fall too frequently, or if water sits too long in one corner of a field, the fungus attacks the roots. Suddenly the plant ages. Green chiles that were ripening stop growing and turn red. No more new fruits form, and the leaves change to a burnt orange, as if frost had hit. "I've seen farmers lose half their crop to wilt," she said.

Plant breeders are developing chiles that resist wilt, but in the meantime, Apodaca-Cervantes, like other Mesilla Valley farmers, plants her chiles in fields as far removed from one another as possible, so that if rain soaks one, it may spare the other.

"Chile wilt almost always hits," she said. "You learn just to hope for it to hit late." With luck, she will be able to pull several pickings of green New Mexico chiles from each plant. Each picking will stimulate the bush to produce more. By October, the final fruits develop. These she allows to turn

Above: Salt covers these Cayenne peppers as they move up towards the crusher, which will turn them into pulp. After aging between six months and two years, the Cayenne mash becomes the basic ingredient in Louisiana-style hot sauces.

Overleaf: Mexican author Arturo Lomelí has collected some lively Mexican proverbs and expressions related to chiles. When people want to scold someone for being too finicky about the exact amount of their share of a bill in a restaurant, fellow diners exhort, "Don't be the sort who counts chiles." When children squirm in their chairs, people say they are "making chiles," because they appear to be grinding chiles with their bottoms. In the still-life arrangement shown here, ground chiles sit in a traditional Mexican grinding basin, the *molcajete,* surrounded by Jalapeños, Cayennes, and New Mexico chiles.

red and sun dry naturally on the vine. When chile wilt attacks at that point, it affects her production figures and her pocketbook much less.

We crossed an irrigation ditch, drove past a patch of Güeritos, and stopped at a broad field of Cayennes. Thirty Mexican harvesters in white hats and long-sleeved shirts knelt among long rows of chile plants. Beneath the thick green foliage dangled long, slender Cayenne peppers. Some remained green; others were red. Unlike long New Mexico green chiles, Cayennes stay on the plant until they turn red.

Sweat ran down the harvesters' faces, but they appeared not to notice. Some talked as they worked. One sang softly. The tractor chugged in a rhythmic bass. But the predominant sound came from chiles plopping into twenty-pound plastic buckets.

When a picker filled his bucket, he would rise and carry it on his shoulder over to the tractor. There he poured the peppers into the holding bin behind the tractor. The crew boss handed him a pay token, and the picker walked back towards the field, as another harvester arrived to empty another bucket. Physically, this work is so difficult that most of us, if we tried it, wouldn't last more than two hours. Yet, coming and going, pouring out their chiles, the perspiring harvesters moved as gracefully and lightly as if they had been players in a carefully choreographed modern dance.

Apodaca-Cervantes ran her hands along the top layer of Cayennes in the bin. "Agricultural researchers keep trying to come up with a mechanical harvester," she observed. "But no machine can tell the difference between a green chile and a red one. We pick chiles the same way today as they did sixty years ago when my father first started farming."

In those days, it was a small operation: ten acres of land that her father and mother farmed together. By 1938 the two had saved enough to buy one hundred acres, but they still worked hard. As a child, Apodaca-Cervantes used to go to town with her mother to sell chiles and other produce. She used to help her mother roast, peel, and hang green chiles to dry on the clothesline. And every night, chiles were an important part of the meal. "My mother fixed chiles with pork, beef, duck, venison. Practically every recipe she had, there were chiles in it." If, for a change, her mother prepared a main dish without chiles, her father would ask, "Is this a meal for a California family or a New Mexico family?" In his eyes, real New Mexicans ate chiles every day.

In the late 1960s, Apodaca-Cervantes took over management of the farms from her father. Today she continues to run them, with assistance from her three grown children.

We went from the field to the processing plant. Across the street rose a twenty-foot-tall statue of a red chile. Now and then, a truckload of chiles would arrive to be weighed. Back behind the offices, at the front of an open-air shed, a conveyor belt carried Cayennes past the sorters: men and women who wore red hard hats, white masks, and green gloves. Their hands darted among the passing Cayennes and pulled away leaves and debris. Then the chiles moved off towards the salter and a machine that crushes them into pulp.

All through the shed, a haze of capsaicinoids hung in the air. Even though I wore a mask, my throat itched. My eyes burned. I coughed and sneezed.

The workers smiled sympathetically with their eyes, but they weren't sneezing. Fifteen million pounds of Cayennes pass in front of them along the conveyor belt and into the crusher each season, and their bodies have adjusted. They breathe capsaicinoids as easily as the rest of us breathe fresh air.

Apodaca-Cervantes led me, still sneezing, to the capsaicinoid-free haven of her office. "The thing about this kind of life is, you have to be able to drive yourself," she said, as she handed me a box of tissues. "I'm always in high gear. I get six hours of sleep a night."

When she isn't talking with her farm foreman, or checking computer figures on her crops, or discussing business questions with her children, or talking with her staff agronomist, she's thinking of what she would like to do next. She would like to find a food processor who would gamble on salsas made from a mixture of red and green chiles. She would like to develop an irrigation system that would reduce the risk of chile wilt. She would like to increase annual Cayenne production to twenty million pounds. And she would like to start joint ventures with businesspeople and farmers in the state of Chihuahua, Mexico.

A few days later, I found her outside her home pinning green chiles on the line to dry. They looked like wrinkled handkerchiefs hanging limp in the sun. When she hugged me goodbye, I could smell the fragrance of roasted chiles in her hair. "I love the land," she said. "It was good to my father and mother, and it's been good to me and my children. There's nothing at all that I'd change. Except maybe I'd like more time for myself. I would like a little time to read."

Other chile farmers I visited work nonstop, too. Take Ed Curry. He runs Curry Farms outside Willcox in southern Arizona, east of last century's popular Santa Cruz Valley. On

Above: Most farmers pick these medium-hot peppers, called Güeros or Yellow Hots, while they remain yellow. Left on the plant, they ripen to red. Like Banana peppers, Güeros are sometimes called Wax peppers because of their waxy look. California plant breeder Paul Smith developed a special variety of Güeros, the Santa Fe Grande, which resists tobacco mosaic virus, one of many diseases that afflict Capsicums.

Right: Chile breeders are trying to develop peppers that can be harvested by machine. The peppers should grow upright, rather than hanging down among the foliage. They should develop in clusters, and they should separate easily from the stem. Paul Bosland has developed the NuMex Bailey Piquíns shown here to meet these requirements. The extremely hot peppers earn 100,000 Scoville Units, or nine on the Official Chile Heat Scale.

Left: Seeds hold the secrets of next year's peppers. Chiles in fields a mile apart have been known to crossbreed. To prevent surprises, farmers often buy seed from people who specialize in growing chiles in isolation. Certified seeds for popular chiles can run up to $700 a pound.

Overleaf: Plant breeder Rob Johnston of Johnny's Selected Seeds in Albion, Maine, developed these peppers, called Calientes, especially for northern gardens. The peppers' genetic ancestors include chiles from northern China. The thin-walled Calientes take only sixty-five days from transplanting to harvest. They also dry well even in humid climates. Their name means "hot" in Spanish. But Johnston says, "It's probably safe to call them a medium-hot pepper. You can put a whole one in a two-quart pot of soup and not make it too hot to eat."

PIQUANCY: THREE PEPPERS
RED HOT CORNBREAD

1 cup yellow cornmeal
3/4 cup flour
1 teaspoon baking soda
3/4 teaspoon salt
1 egg or 2 egg whites
3/4 cup milk
1/2 cup Sizzling Salsa (page 60)
1 Tablespoon canola oil
1 fresh Jalapeño, chopped extra fine
5 ounces grated mozzarella cheese
canola oil for oiling pans

Mix cornmeal, flour, baking soda, and salt well and set aside. Add egg to milk and beat at low speed until well blended. Before measuring salsa, pour off any excess juice. In a separate bowl, combine oil, chopped Jalapeño, and salsa. Pour this and the milk mixture onto the dry ingredients and stir well. Divide the grated cheese into three parts; sprinkle the first into the cornbread mixture and stir until well blended. Repeat with second and third parts until all the cheese is blended in evenly.

Meanwhile, heat an unoiled cast-iron cornstick or cornbread pan in a 425 degree oven. Remove from oven and oil generously with canola oil. If you don't have a cornbread pan, a nine-inch cast-iron skillet will work fine. Or line the bottom of a nine-inch-square glass pan with baking paper and oil the sides of the pan well, but don't heat the pan in advance. For muffins, place paper muffin cups in an unheated muffin pan and spray the inside of the paper cups generously with your favorite nonstick oil spray. Pour the cornmeal mixture into the pans, molds, or muffin cups.

Bake at 425 degrees for about fifteen to twenty minutes or until top turns light brown. (In cast-iron molds, bread will begin to pull away from the sides of the pan.) Makes twelve to fifteen muffins or cornsticks or one skillet of cornbread.

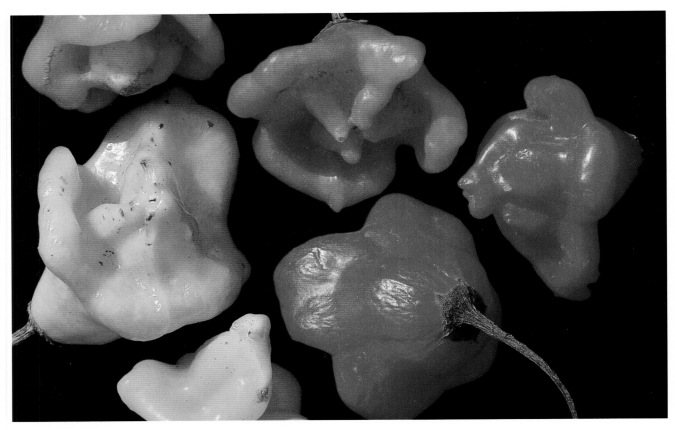

These mildly hot, bell-shaped peppers from Portugal are a rare example of a *Capsicum baccatum* that grows outside the Americas. Scholars believe they developed in Brazil and traveled from there to Europe.

leveled fields beneath the Dragoon Mountains he grows Jalapeños, Poblanos, Pimientos, Cayennes, and yellow Bells.

Early one morning, he let me sit in his office and listen to him talk on the phone so I could get a feel for what his day is like. It was before 7:00 A.M., but he received thirty phone calls or more, in Spanish and English, in as many minutes.

It didn't take me long to see why Curry might not have time to stop and wonder how close to here Coronado passed, four and a half centuries ago. Or daydream about the Apaches who once hid in the hills. Or consider that the roads that connect him with the rest of Arizona and with Mexico follow ancient trails where chile-loving people from the south traveled to meet chile-resistant peoples in the north.

Curry doesn't have time to speak poetically or philosophically about the meaning of chiles and their relationship to humankind. He has to concentrate on why the new cardboard bins don't hold up as well as the last batch. Or whether he can round up enough pickers in time to harvest the chiles before they rot. Or what he's going to do if the storm that's blowing up from the south drops hail on his Jalapeños.

After leaving Curry, I wandered through his chile fields.

Overhead, ravens cawed. Pickers laughed and talked as they dropped chiles rhythmically into buckets. As far as I looked in any direction, chiles in varying stages of development hung red, yellow, and green in the sun. I felt as if I were swimming in chiles, as if I were floating in a metaphysical sea in which the cycles of chiles and the cycles of human life intertwined like passing seaweed.

I bent down and broke off a shining red fruit. What are chiles, really? I asked myself, as I savored the feeling of the heat which spread across my tongue.

They're jumper cables that connect us to other parts of ourselves and each other. They're a reminder and a part of the foolishness of life. And they're a living rope that stretches farther back into the past than we can easily imagine, farther into the future than we can easily see.

Someday, ten thousand years from now, someone will take his first bite of a truly blistering pepper. His eyes will water. He'll begin to sweat. His mouth will feel as if he had just lit a fire inside it. But when the pain passes, a warm tingling will remain. He may not know it, but that fire, and that tingling, will connect him to us, and to that first astonished chile taster so long ago.

Above: Like NuMex Centennial, NuMex Twilight, and several other ornamental *annuums,* these Black Plum chiles are often lumped into the general category of Chinese Multicolor peppers. One of the many pepper mysteries left for future scholars is the origin of that name.

Overleaf: In Mexico, the names Chiltepín and Chile Piquín are interchangeable. In the United States and Canada, Chiltepín usually applies to the tiny, round wild varieties, and Chile Piquín to the larger, elongated varieties. Chile breeders believe that most domesticated *Capsicum annuums* evolved from the elongated form of the wild Piquín. A wild form survived, however, and the chiles shown here represent an example of the recent redomestication of a pepper.

FOR FURTHER READING

Andrews, Jean. *Peppers: The Domesticated Capsicums*. Austin: University of Texas Press, 1984.

Andrews, Jean. *Red Hot Peppers*. New York: Macmillan, 1993.

Berkley, Robert. *Peppers: A Cookbook*. New York: Fireside, Simon and Schuster, 1992.

Bosland, Paul. *Capsicum: A Comprehensive Bibliography*. Las Cruces, New Mexico: The Chile Institute, 1992.

Bosland, Paul W., et al. "Capsicum Pepper Varieties and Classification," *Cooperative Extension Service Circular 530*, College of Agriculture and Home Economics, New Mexico State University, 1992.

Brennan, Georgeanne, and Charlotte Glenn. *Peppers Hot & Chile*. Berkeley: Addison-Wesley (Aris Books), 1988.

Bridges, Bill. *The Great American Chili Book*. New York: Rawson, Wade, 1981.

Butel, Jane. *Chili Madness*. New York: Workman, 1980.

Butel, Jane. *Hotter than Hell: Hot and Spicy Dishes from Around the World*. Los Angeles: Price Stern, 1987.

DeWitt, Dave. *Hot Spots*. Rocklin, California: Prima Publishing, 1992.

DeWitt, Dave, and Paul Bosland. *Pepper Gardening*. Berkeley: Ten Speed Press, 1993.

DeWitt, Dave, and Nancy Gerlach. *Fiery Appetizers*. New York: St. Martin's, 1986.

DeWitt, Dave, and Nancy Gerlach. *The Fiery Cuisines*. Berkeley: Ten Speed, 1991.

DeWitt, Dave, and Nancy Gerlach. *The Whole Chile Pepper Book*. Boston: Little, Brown, 1990.

DeWitt, Dave, and Mary Jane Wilan. *The Food Lover's Handbook to the Southwest*. Rocklin, California: Prima Publishing, 1992.

DeWitt, David A. *Chile Peppers: A Selected Bibliography of the Capsicums*. Las Cruces: The Chile Institute, 1992.

Dooley, Beth. *Peppers Hot and Sweet*. Pownal, Vermont: Garden Way Publishing, 1990.

Fisher, Al, and Mildred Fischer. *Chili-Lovers' Cook Book*. Phoenix: Golden West Publishers, 1984.

Foster, Nelson, and Linda S. Cordell, editors. *Chilies to Chocolate: Food the Americas Gave the World*. Tucson: University of Arizona Press, 1992.

Frank, Lois Allen, with Cynthia J. Frank. *Native American Cooking: Foods of the Southwest Indian Nations*. New York: Clarkson Potter, 1991.

Halász, Zoltán. *Hungarian Paprika through the Ages*, trans. by Lili Halápy. Budapest: Corvina Press, 1963.

Harris, Jessica B. *Hot Stuff: A Cookbook in Praise of the Piquant*. New York: Atheneum, 1985.

Hazen, Janet. *Hot, Hotter, Hottest*. San Francisco: Chronicle, 1992.

Idone, Christopher, with Helen McEachrane. *Cooking Caribe*. New York: Panache Press (Clarkson Potter), 1992.

Kennedy, Diana. *The Cuisines of Mexico*, revised edition. New York: Harper and Row, 1986.

Kerr, W. Park, Norma Kerr, and Michael McLaughlin. *The El Paso Chile Company's Texas Border Cookbook*. New York: William Morrow, 1992.

Long-Solís, Janet. *Capsicum y Cultura: La Historia del Chilli*. México, D.F.: Fondo de Cultura Económica, 1986.

McIlhenny, Paul, with Barbara Hunter. *The Tabasco Brand Cookbook*. New York: Clarkson Potter, 1993.

McLaughlin, Michael. *The Manhattan Chili Company Southwest American Cookbook*. New York: Crown, 1986.

Miller, Mark, with John Harrisson. *The Great Chile Book*, San Francisco: Ten Speed Press, 1991.

Miller, Mark Charles. *Coyote Cafe*. Berkeley: Ten Speed, 1989.

Miller, Mark, and Mark Kiffin. *Coyote's Pantry*. Berkeley: Ten Speed, 1993.

Naj, Amal. *Peppers: A Story of Hot Pursuits*. New York: Knopf, 1992.

Neely, Martina and William. *The International Chili Society Official Chili Cookbook*. New York: St. Martin's Press, 1981.

Peyton, James W. *El Norte: The Cuisine of Northern Mexico*. Santa Fe, New Mexico: Red Crane, 1990.

Quintana, Patricia. *The Taste of Mexico*. New York: Stewart, Tabori and Chang, 1986.

Quintana, Patricia, with Carol Haralson. *Mexico's Feasts of Life*. Tulsa, Oklahoma: Council Oaks Books, 1989

Schweid, Richard. *Hot Peppers: Cajuns and Capsicum in New Iberia, Louisiana*. Berkeley: Ten Speed Press, 1989.

Steele, Louise. *The Book of Hot and Spicy Foods*. Los Angeles: HP Books, 1987.

Stromquist, Joan. *Santa Fe Light and Spicy Recipe*. Santa Fe: Tierra Publications, 1992.

Tolbert, Frank X. *A Bowl of Red*. Garden City, New York: Doubleday, 1966.

Turner, Frederick. *Of Chiles, Cacti, and Fighting Cocks*. San Francisco: North Point, 1990.

Willinksy, Helen. *Jerk: Barbecue from Jamaica*. Freedom, California: Crossing Press, 1990.

ACKNOWLEDGMENTS

Numerous pepper authorities shared their knowledge and insights during the years in which we worked on this project.

Dr. Paul Bosland remained ever patient and helpful and allowed us unlimited access to his gardens and greenhouses. Most of the art photos in this book depict peppers that he grew.

Similarly, Dr. Paul Smith interrupted his own projects repeatedly to identify peppers, clarify technical details, hunt up background material, and offer wise suggestions for improving the book.

Dave DeWitt and Nancy Gerlach of *Chile Pepper* magazine taught us the entertainment value in chiles and generously shared their pepper lore.

Dr. Hardy Eshbaugh helped especially in the final stages of editing.

Dr. Barbara Pickersgill, Dr. Ben Villalon, Dr. Jean Andrews, and Dr. Janet Long-Solís also provided essential assistance.

Our deepest thanks to all of them and to all the farmers, chefs, entrepreneurs, chile aficionados, seed sellers, chili buffs, and others who responded so enthusiastically and supportively to our questions, cameras, visits, and requests.

Finally, special thanks to *Smithsonian* magazine editors Don Moser, Caroline Scott Despard, and Jack Wiley, who started us on the path that led to this book.

Readers who would like to share their anecdotes about peppers with the author may send them to her at P.O. Box 8400, Santa Fe, New Mexico 87504. She regrets that she cannot respond personally.

For information on how to become a member of the Chile Institute, write Box 30003 Dept. 3Q, New Mexico State University, Las Cruces, NM 88003; 505-646-3028.

INDEX

ABOUT THE AUTHOR

Like many other North Americans, Susan Hazen-Hammond began eating chile peppers seriously in the early 1980s. She says, "It didn't take me long to learn a fundamental lesson: The more peppers you eat, the more you want to eat them." She also discovered that the more research she did on peppers, the more she wanted to do. Today she is on the advisory board of the Chile Institute.

A former National Merit Scholar, Hazen-Hammond writes fiction, nonfiction, and poetry from her home in Santa Fe, New Mexico. Her writings, which include more than three hundred articles, reviews, short stories, and poems, have been published around the world. Among her four nonfiction books is *Only in Sante Fe*. She and photographer Eduardo Fuss have traveled on assignments in Europe, South America, Mexico, and the United States. While working in the Yucatan, she took her first bite of the world's hottest pepper, the Habanero. That was several years ago, but she swears her mouth's still burning.

ABOUT THE PHOTOGRAPHER

Shortly after moving to the United States from Argentina in 1963, Eduardo Fuss ate his first chili dog—and fell in love with the tastes of chile peppers. He began photographing peppers seriously in the 1980s, and his art photography of peppers has appeared in such diverse publications as *Smithsonian* magazine and the Danish science magazine *Illustreret Videnskab*. He says, "One reason I like to photograph chiles is because they create a symphony of red for my lens."

A major Italian publication, *Airone*, has called Fuss "A Poet of the Visual Image." His travel and nature photography has been exhibited in galleries in New York, Maine, Connecticut, and Maryland and has been featured in more than a dozen books. This is the fourth book devoted exclusively to his photographs. Formerly the curator of the Joseph Hirshhorn private art collection, he left New York for Santa Fe in 1980.